THEODOR HERZL

Excerpts From His
Diaries

JEWISH POCKET LIBRARY

SCOPUS PUBLISHING COMPANY, INC.
NEW YORK   1941

GRATEFUL acknowledgement is made to The New Palestine for the use of excerpts appearing in the Herzl Memorial Book translated by Maurice Samuel. Acknowledgement is also made to Mr. Mordecai Newman for his selection of passages and to Mr. Joel Lipsky for his translations.

INTRODUCTION

STRANGE—IS IT NOT?—THAT IN A TIME OF DYING FAITH, IN an era when death-chants are intoned for what is noblest and best on earth, there also appear those men on whose shoulders has fallen the mantle of the Prophets. They come upon the scene silently and humbly, seldom recognized, frequently despised and the object of jeers, if not of outright persecution. For the world, set in its ways as it is, resents being disturbed and therefore has no eye and no ear and no heart for the high idealism of the Prophet and for his burning passion for that wondrous life from which rises like a still, white rose the eternal prayer for redemption.

Unaccountable to the multitude, those mysterious figures, whose souls are torn by the sharp pangs of *Weltschmerz*, in turn cannot but feel intensely lonely in the midst of the modern world's din and in that Babel of voices which is our loquacious human race. Even so, the clatter of everyday life distracts them not. Above the universal cacophony they hear in their own hearts the echo of mighty sounds that come welling up from the unplumbed mystic depths and that reverberate against the sounding-board of infinite backgrounds.

And then at last they too raise their voices. They can no longer hold their peace. Something more powerful than themselves compels them to utterance. The multitude may laugh with contempt, it may hound and break them on the pillory, call them fools or denounce them as dangerous revolutionaries; in their own heart—which is the principle of life—they have heard the age-old, ineluctable command: Son of man, prophesy! Prophesy, son of man! Touched by the coal of fire, their lips utter the Word of the Most High. And the sound thereof is like that of many waters, at times like a storm-wind that shakes the pillars of the existing order of things.

Thus they become, though they themselves may perish, the trail-blazers to the coming day, the harbingers of the new spring that must follow the long winter of man's sorrows. Their word it is that causes the sandy walls of proud materialism to sag and melt, the beggars' wisdom of tired souls to appear as folly and the sick illusions of the armed hosts to evaporate like mists in the penetrating light of dawn.

The word that the Prophets announce, the eternal word of redemption, never-dying, always rising again from the depths of forgetfulness, ever restated anew by the true messengers of God, that word is: humanity.

Hitherto we have had only fragments of humanity, as we have had only snatches of peace and particles of art. Humanity cannot emerge so long as we make war one with the other, so long as there exist social inequalities dividing men, no matter what the value of their individual souls, into exploiters and exploited. So long as the reign of violence and force prevails we will be not the masters but the slavish servants of nature. For what characterizes nature is the predominance of force. Man will never escape the thralldom of nature, that is, the servitude of hatred, brutality and ferocity, until he has conquered it in his own bosom, that is to say, until he has created a real fraternal harmony. Then only, when he has done that, will a new bond be established between humanity and nature, and all the unknown and unsuspected tenderness and goodness that slumber in the human heart will become manifest and visible and luminous.

For the creation of the new humanity it is necessary not only that the world be penetrated by the conception of the essential dignity of the human personality, but also by the need and the right of nations to cooperate freely, according to their own character, in a personal-national sense, in the construction of the new earth. Every man must come to recognize that he has two fatherlands, his own and the City of God. Of the first he is an inhabitant, of the second the builder, whose task it is to raise the walls higher and higher above the rivers of hatred and woe that have devastated our world so long.

The Emancipation (of the Jews), decreed at a moment when the high tide of idealism, engendered by the French Revolution, swept over Europe, fell short of being a truly liberating movement for the Jewish people. The French Revolution, it is true, proclaimed the individual, the citizen, as the center and the goal. The human personality was set free. But it did not liberate Jewish life. On the contrary: it isolated and empoverished it. Without question the individual belongs to a vast system. But humanity has no transcendental value. The liberation of the individual is but half-work if the national group to which he belongs is not free or set free at the same time to work out its own destiny.

The Jewish people were not set free in a national sense

by the Emancipation. The Emancipation did not invite
Israel, as a collective unit, to collaborate henceforth in
his own folkish way in the furtherance of the cause of
humanity. It merely provided an opportunity for individual Jews to conform to the general norm of life of the
peoples amongst whom they happened to dwell. It did
not open the road for the Jewish people to contribute out
of the wealth of its own national experience and creative-
ness to the sum total of civilization.

Therefore it is not too much to say that the Emancipation took more—or, rather, demanded more—from the
Jews than it was prepared to give. It asked of them assimilation, surrender of their national ethos, self-
effacement, national death by withholding national self-
determination.

On the other hand, it must be conceded, too, that the
national emancipation of the Jewish people was hampered
a priori by obstacles flowing from the historic circum-
stance of the Dispersion, which had in no small measure
caused the scattered Jewries to lose the idea of nation-
hood. With some Jews their earthly fatherland, Palestine,
had become wrapped up in mystical clouds of unreality.

True, the nostalgia for Zion had never died in the
Jewish people. During all the centuries that had passed
since the destruction of the Judean state by Titus and the
final uprooting of the Jewish people from their homeland
by Hadrian, the prayer for the restoration of the Holy
City had not been stilled in the synagogues of the Galuth.
From time to time, unable to bear the separation any
longer, bands of Jews had returned to Palestine, there to
join the struggling community of pious men and women
in the consoling nearness of the crumbling ruins of the

holy places. The vigil at the dusty remnants of God's house had never been totally abandoned. There were at all times Jews in Palestine to testify by their mere physical presence that they, as a people, had not given up their claim to possess the land of their fathers. But it is also true that the return of these Jewish pilgrims had never assumed the character of a national endeavor, or an effort on the part of a national vanguard.

It was not till Dr. Theodor Herzl, a Viennese journalist residing in Paris as correspondent of the Vienna *Neue Freie Presse*, shocked by the resurgence of militant anti-Semitism in the land of the Declaration of the Rights of Man and of the Emancipation, saw the path that would lead to the Jewish people's salvation. The Dreyfus Affair awakened Herzl to the necessity of creating somewhere on earth a refuge for the Jewish people, a physical refuge and a spiritual rallying center for their drooping national spirit. For if anti-Semitism could rear its ugly head in France, the most civilized of European countries, what could not be expected of Germany and other places if ever nationalist chauvinism should come to the fore in days of national adversity?

A wave of nationalism extending over half a century or more had run through the European continent. Hungary had revolted and loosened the ties that bound it to the Austrian Empire to the extent of achieving cultural autonomy at least. Poland was clamoring to be freed from the onerous Czarist yoke. Italy had known the Risorgimento under Mazzini and Cavour, and in 1871 the troops of Garibaldi had marched through the Piazza del Popolo in the Eternal City to weld the Italian states into one cohesive commonwealth. At the same time the beggars' blanket of Germany's thirty-odd principalities had been forged into the First Reich by Bismarck's diplomacy and Moltke's hammerblows. Belgium had torn itself free from Holland in the late thirties. Even the Slavs of the Balkans had begun to shake off the Ottoman might. Hellas was freed. The Cretans hoisted the banner of independence.

Only the Jewish people remained untouched by the fever of the new nationalism. Jews were dying on all the barricades of freedom. Jewish poets inspired the Poles to revolt, the moujiks to break the feudalism of the Romanoffs, the Spaniards to throw off the medieval obscurantism of the Bourbons. Their own national cause was left unfought.

Theodor Herzl opened that battle with a demand on the civilized world that the Land of Israel, which ages of neglect had turned into a wilderness, be restored to the People of Israel. The demand alone had for effect a beginning of awakening Jewish national consciousness. Herzl did not liberate the Jewish people. Like Moses, he brought them the vision of the Promised Land but himself saw it only from far off. Herzl was the prophet of the national ideal. He gave the scattered and fragmentarized Jewish people one common hope and inspired them to one common task: the redemption of their national homeland.

Personally Herzl went under in the struggle. He died at the age of forty-four of overstrain in his self-imposed double task of convincing the Gentile world and persuading the Jewish people of the necessity of providing a home for a homeless nation. He literally moved heaven and earth, sacrificed his personal wealth, broke off a promising career, fought night and day on the platform, in conference rooms and in the press, against the critics of his plan: the assimilationist Jews, whose tranquillity was disturbed by the prospect of a revivified Jewish nation with whom they might by implication be identified. In the end he ruined his health.

But the idea lived and grew until a new wave of idealism swept through the world at the close of the Great War. This wave, which was set in motion by Woodrow Wilson, projected the doctrine of self-determination for small nations out of the welter and chaos of conflicting national and international interests, and on its crest carried the elementary fabric for the establishment of a Jewish commonwealth in Palestine into the realm of reality.

The Prophet's dream came true. The miracle of a regenerated Jewish Palestine exists today for all the world to see. Not only has Palestine provided a haven of refuge for hundreds of thousands of Jewish refugees from the lands of terror, but the interest taken in the building of Palestine by Jews in the Diaspora has filled their lives with new meaning and content. Judaism as a religious civilization is slowly awakening again after years of torpor and indecision. In the Book of Job it is said that the flower resuscitates by the distant smell of water. In response to the regenerated Jewish life flowing today in Palestine Judaism all over the world begins to function once more as a conscious collaborator, in a personal national sense, in the construction of Olam Haaba, the world to come, to the good of the cause of humanity.

PIERRE VAN PAASSEN

PREFACE

I

THE YEAR 1789 SAW THE ADVENT OF THE FRENCH REVOLU-
tion with its tidings of "liberty, equality, fraternity" to all
mankind. Count forward one hundred and fifty years and
you arrive at the year of grace 1939 and the outbreak of
the present War. The intervening period is crowded with
movements and events of deepest significance to civilization. History ran its course with ever increasing accelera-
tion: from the fall of the Bastille and the proclamation of
the Rights of Man through the Napoleonic era; the spread
of democracy; the rise of nationalism; the triumphal
progress of science; the Industrial Revolution; the growth
of modern Imperialism; the evolution of international
Socialism; the cataclysm of the World War with its after-
math of Bolshevism and Reaction; down to the rise of the
concentration camp, the spread of totalitarianism, and the
suppression of liberty over the major part of Europe.

The modern history of the Jews has been bound up
with these developments. With the fall of the Bastille fell
the walls of the Ghetto. The doctrine of the Rights of
Man was applied with the logical precision of the French
mind to all civilized men, Jews included. The Emancipation of the Jews from oppressive restrictions was imposed
on Western Europe by the triumph of these ideas and the
victory of French arms. The Revolution was the Messiah.
It sounded for the Jews the knell of bigotry, the end of
martyrdom, and announced the dawn of freedom and
reconciliation.

But this freedom did not come to the Jews as a right won by victorious struggle. It was a conditional gift. The boon of equality was extended not to the Jewish People in its corporate capacity but to the Jews as individuals. It was grounded on the assumption that Jewish nationality was non-existent. The price of Emancipation was assimilation and the disappearance of the Jewish People as a distinct entity among the nations. The condition was accepted. A high assembly of French Jewry, summoned by Napoleon, solemnly renounced Jewish national aspirations and reduced Judaism to its purely religious terms. None but a religious bond was to exist henceforth between Jews. The idea was embraced by the Jewries of Western Europe and partly in Eastern Europe as well. Henceforth they would be Frenchmen, Magyars, Germans—of the "Mosaic persuasion." In language, dress and manners—in their very thoughts and sentiments—they would be wholly at one with their fellow countrymen, indistinguishable for all practical purposes from the peoples among whom they dwelt.

II

Though the achievement of complete equality was a gradual process, the Jews adhered faithfully to the bargain they had struck. Assimilation was pursued with religious zeal, degenerating often into sheer flight from the Jewish fold. Avidly Jews seized upon their new-found opportunities, penetrating into every sphere of cultural and economic life. They prospered and rose to eminence. They gave freely of their blood on the field of battle, and contributed imperishable names to science and art, to social progress, to politics and statesmanship. But the intoxicating honeymoon was brief, the millennium unreal.

On the fair flower of Emancipation fell the canker of anti-Semitism. The very speed and thoroughness of Jewish assimilation and the sudden incursion of the freedmen into hitherto forbidden fields produced their reaction. Nor did the growth of the democratic idea prevent the spread of anti-Semitism. In a sense it aided the process by promoting among the several peoples of Europe a heightened sense of their own worth, distinctiveness and national destiny. Abstract democracy found its concrete expression in the national State, in which the Jews enjoyed civil rights but had not acquired "soil and honor." The cry "all power to the people!" translated into realistic terms meant: All power and honor to the ethnic group, united, close-knit, homogeneous in culture and spirit, rooted in its historic soil, jealous guardian of its patrimony—undisputed master in its own Home.

Should this patrimony, created by the toil and blood of generations, now be enjoyed by "aliens" who had not shared in its creation, the upstart children of the Ghetto? The anti-Semites supplied both answer and justification. Little Hamans arose—the authentic precursors of Hitler— preaching the racial inferiority of the Jews and the "menace" they implied to European nations. In Eastern Europe the Jewish masses, steeped in poverty, still groaned under the heel of autocracy. Everywhere Jews were exposed to a general offensive—not as a religious sect or as individuals, but in their secular corporate capacity. The anti-Semites had made a two-fold "discovery": first, that the Jews were a distinct people, characterized by special traits; secondly, that these "Semitic" traits were odious and repugnant to the genius of the "master nations" of Europe. Their activity was subversive; it must be suppressed.

III

A wave of Jewish nationalism swept through Eastern Europe as thousands sought relief by emigration. In the West the "emancipated" Jews reacted partly by minimizing the danger, by lying low; partly by appeals to reason, by sermons on the "brotherhood of man"; by palliatives; by committees to combat anti-Semitism, defense committees, societies against intolerance; by charity; by exaggerated patriotism. Many sought refuge in socialism, incurring the increased hostility of the entrenched upper classes, while the wealthy Jews, who went hand in hand with the conservatives and aristocrats, lent color to the demagogic outcry against the "Jew bankers," the "international financiers," the "enemies of the people."

The Jews were helpless to stem the rising tide. Few realized the full gravity of the danger. Scattered, disunited, buffeted, they drifted toward an unseen vortex. They continued to sail the angry seas in the frail bark of Emancipation, still charting their course by the receding stars of Democracy and Progress but with increasing doubt and waning confidence. And there was no firm hand at the helm. The Jews had given a LaSalle to Germany, a Gambetta to France, a Marx to Socialism, to England—a Disraeli; but *Jewish statesmanship* there was none. There was no Jewish policy, no collective will, no organized force, no leader.

IV

At this fateful moment in Jewish history—midway between the fading dawn of Emancipation and the ripe horrors of our day—an epochal figure arose in Israel. Theodor Herzl was the first Jewish statesman since the destruction of Judaea eighteen hundred years ago. He was destined to fashion a collective will for the Jewish people, to chart a course and to create the organized force for the execution of the policy he advocated.

Viewing the period in retrospect one may well assert that never in modern times has a prophet arisen among his people who saw more clearly or endeavored more nobly to guide them along the road to honor and security. It had been Herzl's chief task to overcome the inertia of centuries and set his people into motion. Persistently he had striven to dispel the mood of helplessness and dull acquiescence in their recurrent fate by breathing into them a new spirit of self-confidence and the will to soil and freedom.

Space does not permit of more than the barest outline of Herzl's meteoric career and its impact upon Jewish history. The story has often been told and become part of the legend and saga of a nation reborn.

In eight years he rose from a position of obscurity in Jewish life to acknowledged and unchallenged leadership of the national cause. Into those stormy years he crowded a lifetime of thought and action transforming the Jewish scene. He founded the World Zionist Organization and gave the Jewish people its first taste of parliamentary life and political self-expression by the institution of the Zionist Congress. Poet and journalist it was he who established the financial instruments of the movement—the Jewish Colonial Trust, the Anglo-Palestine Company and Jewish National Fund. He not only formulated a philosophy of Political Zionism but worked out in minute detail plans and specifications for a future Jewish commonwealth.

From the start, with almost nothing behind him but his own audacity, he negotiated with the crowned heads and responsible statesmen of Europe, playing a complicated diplomatic game with Palestine as its stake. His profound intuition diagnosed the Jewish position in the Diaspora and pronounced it untenable. Indeed with prophetic vision he warned of the storm that was gathering over European Jewry and which has since burst with full fury upon the present generation.

But his allotted span was brief. While at the height of his moral and intellectual powers, at the age of forty-four, he succumbed, exhausted by his feverish activity. "In the midst of life, come unto death".

The history of Zionism since Herzl's death has been largely the projection of his living will. The political triumphs of later years—the Balfour Declaration and the Palestine Mandate—followed upon his earlier vision and preparatory labors. The tree he had planted bore its fruit in due season. His ideas and conception, even phrases of his coining were embodied in international treaties and passed into the public law of nations. Forty years after the publication of his pamphlet, "The Jewish State", the British Government announced its intention of proclaiming a Jewish State—though in only a part of Palestine.

V

Max Nordau, the most eminent of Herzl's lieutenants, described his chief as endowed with a "genius for action", adding that "he was our Disraeli". Unquestionably, Herzl's thirst for action and passion for achievement lift him high above his predecessors and forerunners in Zionism. But, like Disraeli, he was a many-sided genius, as versatile as he was gifted. Patriot, diplomat, statesman, he was also a literary artist of distinction whose name would have descended to posterity as a man of letters had he devoted to his craft the creative energy he lavished upon Zionism. Nevertheless the pen remained his consolation as well as his means of support, and his literary output was voluminous.

It is one of the major sins of omission chargeable to the Zionist movement that Herzl's writings have never been collected and published in full. Probably no other social or political movement of modern times has failed in that elementary duty toward its founder—and itself. In the English language, apart from "The Jewish State" in pamphlet form, not a single volume of Herzl's writings— plays, stories, essays, speeches, articles, letters, memoranda and state papers—is available to the student of Zionism. None has ever come off the press.

This neglect is the more unpardonable since the events of the past few years and the problems of our day give Herzl's utterances a timeliness, a relevance and an immediate urgency difficult to exaggerate. His foresight marks him out contemporary. In his works we find analysis verified by time, prophecies come true, and a solution

not only confirmed by history but dictated by inexorable
necessity.

VI

This modest volume is but a first tentative step in the
right direction. It is made up of selected excerpts from
the complete *Diaries* which Herzl kept from the beginning of his Zionist life to the end. In their pages he faithfully noted things great and small—drafts of important
letters, outlines of speeches, his reactions to men and
events. To their intimacy he confided his inmost thoughts
and feelings—even such wayward and fantastic notions
as flash or flicker through consciousness to die, remembered but for such a record made at the time, catching
them, as it were, on the wing.

In accordance with Herzl's express instructions, the
Diaries were kept under seal and not made public until
twenty years after his death. The original German edi-
tion (itself abridged by certain omissions) appeared in
three volumes running to 1900 closely printed pages.
Supplementing Herzl's public utterances, the Diaries shed
a new light on his personality. By disclosing his inner
struggles, his fluctuating moods, his resentments, his personal worries, they reveal the man and throw his stature
into relief. The Diaries constitute one of the great human
documents of all time.

The excerpts offered here include but a small fraction
of the whole. To be fully appreciated, they should be
read in connection with a biography of Herzl and a study
of his time. But standing quite alone they make fascinat-
ing reading. They afford intimate glimpses of a rich and
sensitive soul. As in an unfolding drama, we witness the

evolution of an idea, the birth of a movement, the growth of a leader. And scattered throughout are priceless gems, aphorisms, paradoxes, suffused with extraordinary charm and grace. Here are words which haunt and linger like that exquisite avowal: "Zionism was the Sabbath of my life".

Thus freighted let this little book be launched upon its voyage, a frail argosy on uncertain seas. Who knows where it will sail, what shores it will touch? Perhaps— is it too vain a hope in a world without truth and reason? —perhaps among the millions of our youth there may be some in whose heart it may find anchorage. Perhaps there will be a few who may be moved by Herzl's voice to share his "regal dream", who may even be stirred to action, to emulation?

In that event the voyage will be accounted a success.

EMANUEL NEUMANN

BOOK ONE

The *Diaries* open with a sort of prelude or invocation. In the grip of an inspiration, Herzl begins to write the *Diaries in Paris*, Pentecost, 1895. The last entry was the second letter to Mr. Jacob Schiff, May 16, 1904.

Begun in Paris; Pentecost, 1895.

I HAVE BEEN OCCUPIED FOR SOME TIME PAST WITH A WORK which is of immeasurable greatness. I cannot tell to-day whether I shall bring it to a close. It has the appearance of a gigantic dream. But for days and weeks it has filled me, saturated even my subconsciousness; it accompanies me wherever I go, broods above my ordinary daily conversations, looks over my shoulder at my petty, comical journalistic work, disturbs me and intoxicates me.

What it will lead to it is impossible to surmise as yet. But my experience tells me that it is something marvelous, even as a dream, and that I should write it down—if not as a memorial for mankind, then for my own delight or meditation in after years. And perhaps for something between both these possibilities; for the enrichment of literature. If the romance does not become a fact, at least the fact can become a romance.

Title: THE PROMISED LAND!——

When was it I began to occupy myself with the Jewish question? Certainly ever since I read Dühring's[1] book. In one of my old notebooks, packed away somewhere in

---

[1] E. K. Dühring, German philosopher with anti-Semitic leanings. He wrote a book "Die Jude—frage als Frage der Rassenschädliche für Existenz, Sitten und Kultur der Volker". 1833–1901.

Vienna, are some of my first observations on Dühring's book and the question. At that time I had not yet found a journal to publish my literary work—it was, I believe, in 1881 or 1882; but I know that even today I often say things that I wrote then. As the years went on, the Jewish question ate its way deeper into me, tormented me and made me very unhappy. In actual fact I returned to it again and again whenever I translated my own personal experience, pain and joy into general terms.

The Jewish question naturally glowered at me from every corner. I sighed over it, I jested, felt unhappy, but I was never thoroughly gripped by it, although even before I came here I wanted to write a Jewish novel. I was going to compose it during my travels in Spain, in 1891. The central figure was to be my dear friend Heinrich Kana, who shot himself in Berlin in February, 1891. I believe that I wanted to exorcise his ghost in the writing of that novel.——

Then the *Neue Freie Presse* called me to Paris as its correspondent. In Paris I entered—at least as an observer—political life. I saw how the world is ruled. I also stood at gaze before the phenomenon of the crowd, for a long time without understanding it. Here I also knew a freer and higher relationship to anti-Semitism, from which I at least did not have to suffer directly. In Austria or Germany I had always to tremble lest some one shout HEP! HEP! after me. Here I passed "unrecognized" in the crowd.

In that word "unrecognized" lies a terrific reproach against the anti-Semites.

Hep! Hep! is the cry which comes down from the Jew-baiting mobs of the Middle Ages. Its origin is said to be the first letters of the three words: Hierosolyma est perdita, Jerusalem is lost.

That HEP! HEP! has come to my own ears only twice. The first time in Mainz, when I traveled through the city in 1888. In the evening I came to a cheap concert hall, drank my beer there, and as I stood up and made my way toward the door through the noise and smoke a young fellow called after me: HEP! HEP!

The second time it was in Baden, when somebody called "Jew-Pig" after me as I went by in a carriage.——

From the beginning I understood the emptiness and futility of efforts to "combat anti-Semitism." With paper declamations or arguments moving in a vicious circle nothing at all can be done. In fact, the effect is comical. You may find—among pushers and cranks—very honest people on such "relief committees." They resemble the "relief committees" which follow—and precede—floods, and are about as far-reaching in effect. The noble Bertha von Suttner[2] is in error—an error, indeed, which does her all honor—when she thinks that such a committee can be of help.

Herzl tells how he tried to win the editor-in-chief of the *Neue Freie Presse* to the idea of a Jewish State and failed. While he sits for the sculptor Beer, in Paris, the inspiration comes. Herzl describes the occasion as follows:

The conversation turned to the fact that it did not help the Jew at all if he were an artist untainted by money. The curse clung. I became greatly excited in my talk, and I was still glowing after I left. With the swiftness of that

[2]Baroness Von Suttner, Austrian writer and pacifist, who was helpful to Herzl in making political connections.

dream in the Arabian fairy story rose the plan for this work. I think I had scarcely gone the distance from the Rue Descombes to the Place Pereire, and it was complete in my mind.

The next day I sat down. Three wonderful weeks of excitement and work.

I thought that through this dramatic eruption I should write myself free. On the contrary, I was drawn in deeper and deeper. The thought grew ever stronger that I had to do something for the Jews. For the time I went to the Temple in the Rue de la Victoire, and again I found the service festive and touching. There was much to remind me of my youth, the Temple on the Tabakgasse in Budapest.

Did it happen then? Or had I conceived before that time the plan to write "The Situation of the Jew?"

I remember now that it was on an earlier occasion. I had already spoken of it in Vienna during the autumn. I had planned to study Jews wherever the accidents of world history had scattered them—Russia, Galicia, Hungary, Bohemia, then the Orient, the new colonies in Zion, and finally western Europe again. My faithful, factual description would make the misfortunes of the Jews clear and show that they were undeserved.

Before Easter one day I had a conversation with Alphonse Daudet.[3] He happened to mention the Jews. He admitted that he was an anti-Semite. I explained my point of view to him and found myself growing enthusiastic again. When I told him I wanted to write a book for and

[3] Alphonse Daudet, the French novelist.

about the Jews, he said, "A novel?" "No," I answered. "A book for men."

But he insisted, "A novel goes further. Think of *Uncle Tom's Cabin.*"

I continued to expound my ideas until he too, was interested and at last said, "How beautiful! How beautiful!"

How I came from the ideas that I intended to express in the novel to plans for practical work, is still a mystery to me, even though this took place during the last few weeks. It happened in the subconscious.

Suddenly one day I wrote a letter to Baron de Hirsch[4] who has concerned himself with the Jews so remarkably and after the fashion of a great millionaire. After I finished the letter I let it lie for two weeks. Then I looked at it again and finding it not foolish, sent it off.

After some correspondence between Herzl and Baron de Hirsch, which is reproduced in the *Diaries*, they meet in Paris on June 2, 1895. Herzl lays his plans for a Jewish state before the Baron, saying in part:

"You will consider parts of what I am going to tell you too simple and others too fantastic. But people are led by what is simple and fantastic. It is astonishing—and well-known—with what little understanding the world is governed.

Now I never had the slightest inclination to occupy myself with the Jewish question. Nor did you ever think originally of becoming a patron of the Jews. You were a banker, engaged in important affairs; and now

[4]Baron Moritz von Gerenth de Hirsch, founder of "ICA"—Jewish Colonization Association. Its purpose was to colonize Jews in the Argentine. He invested £10,000,000 in that project.

finally you are applying your time and your money to the cause of the Jews. And I also was by nature a writer and journalist, never giving a thought to the Jews. But my experience and observations, and the growing pressure of anti-Semitism forced me into the service of the cause.

I shall not go into the history of the Jews, with which I wanted to begin. It is well-known. But I must emphasize one thing. Throughout our two thousand years of dispersion we have never had any unified leadership in our political life. I regard this as our principal misfortune; that is what has harmed us more than any persecution. That is what has ruined us internally, and destroyed us. For there was no one who could train us to be straightforward men. We were pushed into every kind of vicious trade, and held down in the Ghetto where we decayed among ourselves; and when we were let out people wanted us to have the habits of freedom all at once.

But if we had a unified political leadership, whose necessity need be proven no further, and which is by no means to represent a secret society—if we had this leadership we could apply ourselves to the solution of the Jewish problem. And do that from above and from below and from all sides.

And the end we shall wish to pursue, when we have such a center or head, will determine the means.

Two ends are possible. Either to remain or to emigrate.

For either, the same kind of popular education will be necessary, because even if we emigrate it will be a long time before we come into the Promised Land. Moses needed forty years. We may need twenty or thirty. In any case new generations will come up in the meantime, which we shall have to train for ourselves.

Now I wish to begin from the very outset with quite different methods of training from yours.

First of all there is the principle of philanthropy, which I consider completely fallacious. You are breeding shnorrers. It is characteristic that no other people has so much philanthropy and so much beggary as the Jews. The impression is forced on one that there must be a connection between the two phenomena, in such a way that the character of the people is ruined by philanthropy."

He interrupted me: "You are quite right."

I continued:

"Years ago I heard that your experiments with the Jews in the Argentine are producing no results or bad ones.——

But in any case the project should never have been begun as you did it. You drag these agricultural Jews all the way over there, and they must think that they have a further right to your support, and it is just this which doesn't help the will to work. Whatever such an export-Jew costs you he's not worth it. And how many specimens can you send over there anyhow? Fifteen—twenty thousand! More than that live in one alley of the Leopoldstadt[5] in Vienna. No, direct means are quite inapplicable for moving masses of people. You can only be effective with indirect ones.

Even if your twenty thousand Argentinian Jews do well, you will not have proved anything. But if they fail, you will be furnishing terrible evidence against the Jews.

[5]The Jewish Quarter in Vienna.

With your twenty thousand Argentinian Jews you still can't prove anything, even if they do well. But if it's a failure then you are presenting a terrible testimony against the Jews.

Enough of criticism. What is to be done?

Whether they stay or migrate, Jewish masses must first of all be improved in the very places they are now. They must be put in fighting trim, made happy at their work and virtuous. And emigrate later—if it's necessary.

For this improvement you can make better use of your means than you have up to now.——

Instead of buying the Jews for yourself one by one, establish gigantic prizes in the principal anti-Semitic countries: for actions d'eclat, for conduct of great moral beauty, for courage, self-sacrifice, ethical behavior, great achievements in art and science, for the physician during an epidemic, the warrior, the discoverer of a cure, of some public benefit, it doesn't matter what,—in short, for everything great.

Two things will be attained by the prizes: first of all general amelioration, and secondly publicity. Just because the project is unusual and brilliant everybody will be speaking of it everywhere. In this way people will learn that there are also good Jews, and how many of them.

But the first thing is the more important: the amelioration. The question is not of the individual annual prize-winner. I think the others are more important, who reach up in order to get the prize. In this way the moral level will be elevated."——

Then he said in a benevolent tone of voice, as though I had asked him for an appointment in his banking house:

"I can see that you're an intelligent person."

I only smiled to myself. Such things as my project are beyond self-love. I shall yet see and hear a diversity of things.

And Hirsch finished off his praise: "But you have such fantastic notions."

At that I got up: "Well, didn't I tell you before that this would appear too simple or too fantastic to you? You have no idea what the fantastic is, and that people's great traits can only be observed from a height."

He said: "Emigration would be the only thing. There are enough countries to be bought."

I almost cried out: "Yes, but who has told you that I do not want emigration. Here it is, in these notes."——

Hirsch said: "Where will you get the money? Rothschild will subscribe five hundred francs."

"The money?" I said, laughing and contrary. "I shall collect a national Jewish loan of ten billion marks."

"Fantasy!" the Baron smiled. "The rich Jews won't give a thing. The rich are bad, they have no interest in the sufferings of the poor."

"You are speaking like a socialist, Baron Hirsch!"

"And I am one. I'll be ready in a moment to give away everything if the others will have to do it too."——

From a letter to Baron Hirsch, June 3, 1895.

——I spoke of an army, and you interrupted me even as I began to speak of moral training for marching. I allowed myself to be interrupted. Nevertheless I have already sketched out the rest of it. The whole plan. I know everything that goes with it. Money, money, money: means of evacuation, care of great masses of people (which is to be understood not merely as food and drink, as in Moses's simple time), maintenance of discipline, the organization of departments, emigration contracts with the heads of states, transit contracts with others, guarantee agreements with everybody, and the fitting out of magnificent new dwelling places. All this must be preceded by propaganda, the popularization of the idea through papers, books, brochures, lectures on emigration, pictures, songs. Everything directed from one centre, with far-sightedness and full consciousness of the goal. But I should finally have had to tell you what our flag would be and how I want to unroll it. And then you would have asked me mockingly: A flag? What is that? A pole with a scrap of cloth?—No, my dear sir, a flag is more than that. With a flag you can lead people wherever you want, even into the Promised Land.

For a flag they will live and die; it is even the only thing for which they are prepared to die in numbers, when they are trained to it.——

As a practical matter the exodus into the Promised Land represents a vast transportation project unparalleled in the modern world. What is transportation? A complex of all human enterprises, enmeshed in each other like cogs of a wheel. And even in the first stages of this undertaking the crowds of our aspiring youth will find employment: all the engineers, architects, technicians, chemists, physicians, lawyers, who have come out of the Ghetto in the last thirty years and believed that they would find their bread and their little bit of honor outside of petty Jewish trading affairs; who now find themselves desperate and are beginning to constitute a frightful educated proletariat, but to whom all my love belongs, and whose numbers I want to multiply just as you want to diminish them, in whom I see the future and still slumbering strength of the Jews. In a word, my own sort.

And out of these educated proletarians I shall build the general staff and the cadres of an army that will seek the land, find the land and conquer the land.——

Believe me: the politics of an entire people—particularly when it is scattered throughout the whole world—can be made only with imponderabilia, which float in the air. . . . What? You do not understand the imponderable? And what is religion? . . .

Yet the national fantasy must have firm ground beneath. But who says that I have not thoroughly practical ideas as to the detailed method?——

What are ten billion marks for the Jews?—— As a matter of fact, under pressure of necessity we could start off with one billion. For it will be working capital, the foundation of our later railways, our immigration fleets and our war fleet. With this we shall build houses, palaces, workers' dwellings, schools, theatres, museums, government houses, hospitals, lunatic asylums—in brief, cities.

You will find Jewish money in great quantities for a Chinese loan, for negro railways in Africa, for most adventurous enterprises. Is it possible that for the deepest, most immediate and most tormenting needs of the Jews you will find none?

As is well known, the negotiations with Hirsch came to nought. The next section of the *Diaries* is a series of fragments of ideas, which Herzl intends to integrate with the *Judenstaat*.

Fragmentary Thoughts Relating to "The Jewish State"

General sanitary measures must be taken before masses entrain. We shall have emigrant hospitals (quarantines), baths, clothing institutes before emigration.

*   *   *

To try to prepare, artificially, a historic peasantry is like equipping a modern army with bows and arrows.

*   *   *

I am so filled with this idea that I refer everything to it, as a lover refers everything to his beloved. . . .
Order of procedure:

1. Creation of means (the syndicate).
2. Beginning of publicity (which costs nothing, for the anti-Semites will be happy, and I shall break the opposition of liberals by threat of competition).
3. Engagement of land prospectors.
4. Continuation of publicity on a grand scale. Let Europe laugh at it, swear at it—as long as it talks about it.
5. Negotiations with Zion.
6. Marking out of territorial points to be acquired.
7. Purchase of first lands (one billion).
8. Purchase and construction of ships.
9. Continuous enrollment of all who report; recruiting, division, direction——

*   *   *

The cowardly, assimilated, baptized Jews may remain. Even they will come in useful—they will be proud of their relationship with us, of whom they are now ashamed. But we, the faithful Jews, will again become great.

*   *   *

Equal rights are included in the laws, but in fact they have been suspended.

*   *   *

We produce too much intelligence and no longer have a market for it.——

*   *   *

Municipal lay-out: First, canals, water, gas, etc., then wooden stories above.

We shall not only copy Paris, Florence, etc., but look for a Jewish style also, expressing relief and freedom.

Open cheerful hallways, borne on columns.

Make air zones between cities. Every city like a large house situated in a garden.

*   *   *

My perpetual concern must be a sound economy. No squandering, no waste. This is no trough for gluttons and slackers.

*   *   *

No taxes as long as possible, or at most indirect ones which do not touch the belongings of the little man.——

*   *   *

These notations prevent me from setting down what went before in my book.

In the draft copy, I am still at the conversation with Hirsch.

But the growth of the new thoughts which occur to me is more important. Who knows how soon it will be over?

At the same time I feel the anxiety portrayed by Heine in that wonderful little poem about the artist:

> "*I tremble*
> *Lest I may pass away this night,*
> *Pass away before I bring this work to a close.*"

*   *   *

The flag has occurred to me. Perhaps a white flag with seven golden stars. And the white field stands for our new clean life. The stars symbolize the seven-hour working day we shall institute. Under the sign of labour we go into the Promised Land.

*   *   *

Much that is set down in these notes will appear ridiculous, exaggerated, crazy. But if I were to exercise self-criticism, as in my literary works, the thoughts would become crippled. Artists will understand why, amid my practical political and law-creating ideas I, who am for the rest clear in my logic, permit these exaggerations and dreams to spout like green grass between cement stones. I must not force myself downward into a state of sober carefulness. This light intoxication was necessary.

Yes, the artist will understand it completely. But there are few artists.

Page after page these random ideas continue. They touch on every imaginable theme. Prizes for large families, disposition of unskilled labour, its organization into an army; architecture, punishments, a House of Lords, general parliamentary organization. In the midst of those reflections he writes to Rabbi Güdemann of Vienna (1835–1918), without unfolding his plan. He wants Güdemann to meet him in Caux—there he will speak to him about the project in detail. The meeting never took place.

The reflections continue in the same irregular stream. Universal insurance; tobacco and whisky monopoly; transformation of the Society of Jews into the Jewish State; religious toleration; building credits; the seven-hour day, etc., etc.

Now follow some extraordinary passages which indicate the struggle which Herzl had to pass through before he could become involved, with all his life, in the realization of his plans.

June 18, 1895. From a letter to Baron de Hirsch.

"My last letter calls for a closing note. I send it now. I have given up the thing. Why? My plan will fail with the poor rather than with the rich Jews. . . .

"Recently I read my plan to a sensible friend of mine (who is not a money man). At first he became as soft as a child; his face was bathed in tears; his intelligence was captured, his heart shaken.

"Then he recovered slowly and said to me: 'With these things you will make yourself either tragic or comical.' The tragic side would not frighten me. But as to the comic side, it would not be I, but the plan itself, that would perish. The worst they could say to me is that I am a poet. That is why I am giving it up.

"For the time being the Jews cannot be helped. If one were to show them the Promised Land, they would despise one."—

June 13, 1895. From an undelivered speech to the Rothschilds.

——Any improvement in the Jewish position is excluded by the above compelling reasons. If anyone asks me how I know this I'll tell him that I also know where a stone that rolls over a steep cliff comes to rest, that is, all the way down. Only ignoramuses or lunatics do not take natural laws into account.

So we Jews, too, must go down, all the way down. Exactly how that will happen, what form it will take, I have no idea. Will it be revolutionary expropriation from below, or will it be reactionary confiscation from above? Will they drive us out? Will they kill us?

I suppose more or less that it will take all these and other forms besides.

The social revolution will come about in one country, and its first victims will inevitably be the Jews.

In Russia there will simply be a confiscation from above.

In Germany they will make emergency laws as soon as the Kaiser cannot do business with the Reichstag.

In Austria they will let themselves be intimidated by the Viennese mob and surrender the Jews. That is, in Austria the street rabble can put through anything, if it desires it. Only the street rabble does not know it yet. The leaders will instruct it soon enough.

So they will drive us out of these countries and kill us in the others, where we take refuge.

Is there then no salvation?

Yes, gentlemen, there is a way which was tried once before. We must repeat a very old, very famous, and thoroughly tested experiment. But in a different, modern, and more refined form. All the means of the present day can be utilized for this simply and easily understandable object.

This simple, ancient experiment is the exodus from Mitzraim.——

The Jewish state is inevitable, gentlemen, and it will come into being either with you or without you.

In the Promised Land we shall have crooked noses, red or black beards and bow-legs without being despised as a result.

In the Promised Land we shall finally come to live upon our own soil and die peacefully in our own homeland. We also as free men shall achieve honor as a reward for great deeds, and we shall live in peace with all the world, which we shall have freed with our freedom, enriched through our riches, and made great through our greatness.

So that the contemptuous epithet "Jew" will become a term of honour, like "Englishman," "Frenchman," "German," in short, like the names of all civilized peoples.

So that we, through our state, shall be able to educate our people at tasks which lie beyond our field of vision at present.——

Now it may seem that this will be a very lengthy matter. I keep on speaking of months, years, and decades. And in the meantime the Jews in thousands of places are being mocked, tormented, beaten, plundered, inveighed against and slain.

No, gentlemen, this is an instantaneous solution. In the twinkling of an eye I shall bring anti-Semitism throughout the world to a standstill. This means the conclusion of peace.——

BOOK TWO

The first book takes up over two hundred pages of the German original, and covers the period from spring of the year 1895 until June 23rd of the same year, when the second book begins.

Herzl begins to evolve plans for putting his project before the Kaiser, Wilhelm II. At the same time he continues to set down fragmentary ideas regarding the Jewish State.

July 6, 1895.

YESTERDAY I SAT DOWN TO A BEER WITH NORDAU. NATURALLY we spoke about the Jewish question. Never have I harmonized so well with Nordau. Never have I noticed so strongly that we belong together. We took the words out of each other's mouths.——

Herzl writes to Güdemann again. He advises him that he has prepared a memorial to the German Kaiser. Meanwhile he is on the look-out for men to interest in his project.

July 22, 1895.

Note on national psychology.

In the Taverne Royale there are some managers who really act as head-waiters. Excellent arrangement! When such a head-waiter, who does not wear a waiter's jacket, hands the guest his plate, the latter feels flattered, chosen for distinction. I have noticed it in myself. In the same way the emigrants to my homeland will have to receive special attention. Jews—as a despised people—are *koved*-hungry—and they must be led thereby.

September 20, 1895.

Beginning of September I left Aussee for Vienna. My first conversation with Bacher [one of the chiefs on the *Neue Freie Presse*], which I had with him on the day of my return, showed me at once that he was absolutely unreceptive to my idea, and that he would perhaps fight it decisively. Thereupon I gave my conversation a theoretical turn.

Bacher considers the anti-Semitic movement transitory, though "uncomfortable."——

By means of Güdemann I came to place the matter before Dr. Ehrlich, a journalistic financial expert.—— Result: he was captured, deeply shaken, did not consider me at all crazy, and really had no financial-technical or politico-economic objections to offer.

Herzl makes a journey to Salzburg to become acquainted with Leven, from whom he learns for the first time about the Zionist movement.

Leven[6] was of the opinion that I should find many supporters in Russia. A certain man Pinsker[7] had lived in Odessa, and had struggled for the same idea—the rehabilitation of a Jewish homeland. Pinsker is unfortunately dead. His writings, said Leven, were marvelous. I must read them as soon as I have time.

Another Jew in England, a Colonel Goldsmid, is also an enthusiastic Zionist; he had wanted to charter ships to conquer Palestine.

[6]A member of the Alliance Israelite in Paris.
[7]Author of "Auto-Emancipation."

October 18, 1895.

Yesterday I spoke for three hours with bank-director Dessauer, and I won him! He considers the migration of the Jews by means of the Bank quite possible. The Rothschilds were not to be counted on. He thought it best to start the Society of Jews with only four million pounds, and issue further bonds later.

I told him: I should rather do nothing at all. A gradual infiltration of Jews will—as always—soon awaken anti-Semitism.

November 17, 1895.

The French Jews are apparently not to be won over to the idea. They are still too comfortable.

Herzl's next big attempt is to win over Benedict, another of the heads of the *Neue Freie Presse*. He sets great store by this. But the *NFP* is not to be won.

November 19, 1895.

Nordau[8] seems to be won for the thing . . .

He believes the plan will need three hundred years for its realization.

I believe thirty—if the idea breaks through.

The center of action has shifted to London.——

The chief Rabbi Dr. Adler, advised me against the Maccabaeans—they were young people, without influence. It would be better if I tried Lord Rothschild and others. He gave me a letter of introduction to Sir Samuel Montague.——

Then comes the first English episode. Herzl visits Zangwill and holds his first semi-public speech on the subject of the *Juden-*

[8]Dr. Max Nordau, author and critic.

staat—before the Maccabaean Club of London. A résumé of the *Judenstaat* is published in the *Jewish Chronicle*.

November 25.

A visit to Colonel Goldsmid.

——In the afternoon I read the plan to the Colonel. He doesn't understand German well.——

But he said: "That is the idea of my life."

He showed me the flag of the Chovevei Zion: the symbols of the twelve tribes. As a counter I unfurled my white flag with the seven stars.——

After dinner, when the ladies and the other English colonel who had been invited were in the salon, I went into the smoking-room with Goldsmid. And then came the astonishing story.

"I am Daniel Deronda," he said. "I was born a Christian. My father and mother were converted to Christianity. When I learned of this as a young man in India I decided to go back to my ancestral people. As lieutenant I went over to Judaism. My family was enraged by it. My wife was also a Christian of Jewish descent; I took her away, first had myself engaged to her in Scotland again, then she had to be converted to Judaism, and we were married in a synagogue. I am an orthodox Jew. This hasn't hurt me in England. My children Rachel and Carmel have been brought up in a strictly religious way, and learned Hebrew quite early."——

Like Montague he is also thinking of a greater Palestine.——

Benedict tries hard to persuade Herzl to withdraw publication of *Der Judenstaat*.

February 3, 1896.

How right I was when I told my parents this afternoon that I am in the midst of the fight now. The fight is between me and the *Neue Freie Presse*, between the employee and the chief. He has the power of his superior position; I have right on my side.

If they force me out of the editorial offices, I must immediately have another paper at my disposal.

I am risking a great deal—my entire position and the *Neue Freie Presse* too.

Herzl now begins to foresee the ridicule as well as opposition he will meet. But he proceeds with the publication of the *Judenstaat*, refusing to yield to Benedict. On February 15th the first copies are on sale in Vienna.

March 2nd.

Herman Bahr (a noted Austrian novelist) paid me a visit. The Jews of the upper-class educated circles, who used to constitute the literary salons, the Bauernfeld nest, and the Grillparzer chorus of the older Vienna, are horrified by me, Bahr says.

That was to be expected.

Jewish student bodies in Vienna approach Herzl. They are among his first supporters. Various other Zionist organizations communicate with him. Herzl does not decide as yet to launch into public action. He is still waiting.

March 10th.

The Reverend William H. Hechler, the chaplain of the local English embassy, visited me.——

Hechler declares that my movement is a "biblical" one,

even though I am going about everything in a rational way.

He wants to have my work sent to a few German princes. He was tutor in the Grand Duke of Baden's house, knows the German Kaiser, and believes he can get me an audience.

April 10, 1896.

A *Privatgelehrter* by the name of Carl Bleicher came to see me. At first I thought he was a *schnorrer* who wanted a small contribution for a book of his own. But he would take nothing, and placed himself at my disposal as propagandist. I note this because it is a sign of the way the poor have been gripped. This poor old man, who lives on gifts of small coins, opened his purse, showed me what he had, and refused my offer. This is the most important difference between my effect on the people and that of Baron de Hirsch. They beg from him but do not love him. I am loved by the beggars. That is why I am the stronger.

On March 17th the *Diaries* record the fact that Herzl was examined by a doctor and his health was found to have been affected by the excitement.

Beginning diplomatic work.

April 14, 1896.

The English pastor Hechler came to me this afternoon in great excitement. He was at the court, where the German Kaiser arrived to-day, and spoke with the general superintendent, Dryander, and with others of the Kaiser's suite. He went walking with them for two hours in the city and told them of the contents of my pamphlet, which astonished them greatly. He said to them that the time had come "to fulfill prophecy."

April 21, 1896, *at night.*

I wanted to go to Pest to-morrow. Late in the evening I got Hechler's call to Karlsruhe.

BOOK THREE

On Sunday, April 22, 1896, Herzl is on the Orient Express, enroute to his first appointment with a European prince to discuss the Jewish question.

A lovely, charming day. A tinge of green on the delightful meadows. The trees are coming out on a woody hill, so that it looks like the top of a broad head. Through them you can see the delicate background of the pale spring sky again—and at this moment I have to be thinking of the dead Baron de Hirsch.——

Karlsruhe, April 23, 1896.

ARRIVED HERE ELEVEN O'CLOCK LAST NIGHT. HECHLER MET me at the station.

He told me the circumstances. The Grand Duke wanted first to have in hand the report of the councillor on the *Judenstaat*.

Hechler showed the Grand Duke the Prophetic Tables —which, it appeared, made an impression. Hechler, in excellent mood, said: "Mark this beautiful day, this gentle spring sky over Karlsruhe! Perhaps one year from to-day we shall be in Jerusalem." Hechler said he would ask the Grand Duke to accompany the Kaiser next year to the dedication of the Church in Jerusalem. I was to be there too, and Hechler would go along as the scientific companion of the Grand Duke.

On entering the palace I tried to divert the power of

the impression by making, like a report, a regular inventory of what I saw: green plush furniture, the brown curved wood of the chair-legs, covered with light gold: photographs of the three Kaisers.

Fortunately Hechler kept chattering incessantly. . . .

Suddenly the door of the apartment opened, and an old, solid, but not stout-looking general entered: the Grand Duke. He is seventy years old, but looks from six to eight years younger.——

At the beginning I spoke with some embarrassment. I thought it best in a lower voice, so that the usual self-intoxication of speech disappeared. After the first friendly question as to my journey and my quarters, I told him what I was by profession, and explained my previous position on the paper in Paris.

The Grand Duke said: "I get the *Neue Freie Presse*." He inquired after Paris, and I described the parliamentary crisis, and in particular the present Bourgeois cabinet.

After a few minutes he interrupted me: "We want to speak of other matters."

Whereupon I plunged at once into the subject, and begged him to interrupt me with questions whenever my exposition was not clear.

So I unrolled the entire question. Unfortunately I was compelled to concentrate so closely on what I was saying, that I was unable to observe him closely. Hechler said later that the conversation should have been taken down in shorthand.—— After that strain of two and a half hours I was so weakened that I can no longer remember the exact course of the conversation.

In any case, the Grand Duke took my creation of the Jewish State in utmost seriousness. His principal worry was that if he were to declare himself for the thing it might be regarded as anti-Semitism.

I explained to him that only those Jews would go who wanted to.

It was his opinion that the governments could take the matter up properly only when they had the Society of Jews to deal with.

I naturally spoke in the contrary sense. Let a few princes first declare themselves favorably: then the Society of Jews would from the outset have more authority. And authority was necessary if the great move were to be made in an orderly fashion. The Jews had to be educated and disciplined to the idea of the migration.

The Grand Duke then turned toward Hechler: "The co-operation of England and Germany on this matter is unlikely enough. Relations are just now unfortunately disturbed. Will England help?" I said: "The English Jews must look after that."

The Grand Duke, somewhat distrustful, said: "If they can." I said: "When it is known that the Grand Duke of Baden is interested in the matter, it will make a profound impression."

He said, quickly: "That is not so. My position is not big enough. Yes, if the German Kaiser, or the King of Belgium were to do it."

I stood firm: "Yes, if an experienced prince, who helped to create the German Empire, and whose advice is now sought by the German Kaiser, were to declare himself on the side of this new enterprise, it would make a tremendous impression. Your Majesty is the adviser of the Kaiser."

He smiled: "I advise him and he does what he likes."

Then he asked me whether I had yet taken any steps with the Sultan.

I answered, thinking of Newlinsky, that someone had offered to speak to the Sultan for me.

I then explained the advantages which the plan had for the Orient. If Turkey were going to be partitioned within a reasonable length of time we could create in Palestine an *état tampon*. In the event of Turkey's enduring we could still contribute a great deal. We could definitely settle the problem of the national budget of the Sultan in exchange for this territory, which was not of much use for him.

The Grand Duke asked whether it would not be better first to bring a couple of hundred thousand Jews to Palestine, and then raise the question.

I said, in a decisive tone: "I am opposed to that. For then the Jews would have to rise against the Sultan as insurgents. I want to do everything openly and clearly, within absolutely legal limits."

At first the Grand Duke looked at me in astonishment when I spoke so energetically; then he nodded his approval, and said: "It would also solve the Egyptian question. England hangs on to Egypt because she must defend her road toward India. Actually Egypt costs more than it is worth."

Finally the Grand Duke said again: "I should like to see it happen. I believe it would be a blessing for many people."

April 26, Vienna.

When I got on to the Orient Express yesterday afternoon in Munich, Hechler was sitting there.——

He unfolded his Palestine maps in the carriage and instructed me for hours. In the north the boundary was to be the mountains opposite Cappadocia, in the south the Suez Canal. Our slogan to be: Palestine as in the time of David and Solomon!——

From a Letter to the Grand-Duke of Baden.

——The thought of my sitting opposite one of the cofounders of the German Reich, the counselor and friend of three Kaisers, made me ill at ease. Nevertheless the cause must not be harmed by the weakness of its representative.——

If God wills that we return to our historic fatherland, then as culture-bearers of the West we should like to bring the cleanliness, order, and enlightened customs of the Occident into what is now a desolate and diseased corner of the Orient.

The details are indicated in my work "The Jewish State." There is also an account there of how the economic damage to the countries which are to be left can and must be forestalled.——

In any case a thoroughgoing evacuation is not being thought of. The Jews already absorbed or who can still be absorbed will remain. The exodus is voluntary and will be felt by the reasonably enlightened Jews not as an expulsion but as an act of grace on the part of the prince.——

May 7, 1896.

This evening I had my wife's cousin explain the financial situation of Turkey to me.

As far as I can see now, the financial plan will have

to consist of the following: the elimination of the European Control Commission, payment of interest on the debt by our Jewish leadership, so that the Sultan may get rid of this control and be able to make fresh loans *ad libitum.*

May 12, 1896.

Great things do not need to have a firm foundation. An apple must be put on the table so that it should not fall. The earth swims in space.

In the same way I may perhaps found and secure the Jewish State without a firm hold on anything.

The secret lies in movement. I believe that on this principle the steerable airship will ultimately be invented. Weight must be overcome by motion: not the ship, but the movement, must be steered.

May 18, 1896.

Nordau reports that he went to see Edmund Rothschild with Zadoc.[9] The "audience" lasted 63 minutes, during which Rothschild spoke for 53 and Nordau, "with difficulty and rudeness," only ten.

Rothschild has absolutely no desire to hear anything of the project; he doesn't think there is anything to be attained through the Sultan, and in any case does not want to give any assistance. He thinks what I'm doing is dangerous because I place Jewish patriotism under suspicion, and harmful—to his Palestinian colonies.

Accordingly we shall go beyond him to the day's agenda.

[9]Zadoc Kahn, chief Rabbi of Paris.

It is entertaining after this to read the reports in to-day's Paris dispatches of street-demonstrations against the Jews and particularly against the Rothschilds. In front of the same house in the Rue Lafitte where Rothschild turned away my friend Nordau on Friday, the people cried out on Sunday: "Down with the Jews!"

The following excerpts from a conversation with Newlinsky indicate the measure of Herzl's ideas.

Without preparation I told Newlinsky[10] that we imagine that Palestine would be given to us for twenty million pounds (one hundred million dollars).

We should use the £20,000,000 for the regulation of Turkey's finances. Two million would be given to Palestine on the basis of the capitalization of its present yield of £80,000 annually. With the other £18,000,000 we should free Turkey from the Control commission.

Herzl is now engaged on his first negotiations with the Sultan. Sets out for Constantinople. The train stops at Sofia where a great crowd of Bulgarian Jews comes to meet him. The Sultan's first Secretary, Izzet Bey, is opposed to the plan. In spite of his determination Herzl fails to see the Sultan during his visit to Constantinople, but does not give up.

July 1, 1896.

Baden, near Vienna

Even the last day in the railway carriage Newlinsky was full of ideas.——

He had the following inspiration:

It ought to be suggested to the Sultan that he au-

[10]Michael von Newlinsky, director of "Correspondence de l'East" —who was to obtain for Herzl the first audience with the Sultan of Turkey.

thorize the Zionist movement to state on his behalf to all Jews that he would open Palestine to them as a principality, with their own laws, army, etc., under his *suzerainty*. For this the Jews would pay a tribute of one million pounds per annum.

I find this idea excellent. I had already been thinking of something similar in Constantinople, but I said nothing about it. It is an acceptable proposition, and up to the present I had to make unacceptable propositions because I was not sure that the people in London would not ditch me at the last moment.

Now I shall go with this proposition to London, where they await me with some excitement.

Herzl speaks with Sir Samuel Montague who, together with Goldsmid, seems to be the most promising material.

London, July 8, 1896.

I told Montague of the practical results from the Grand Duke to the Sultan.

He was moved and soon became enthusiastic.

A wonderful old man.——

London, July 15, 1896. *After a mass meeting in the East End.*

On Sunday, while I sat on the Platform, I was in a curious mood. I saw and heard the rising of my legend. The people are sentimental; the masses do not see clearly. I believe that even now they no longer have a clear idea of me. A light mist has begun to beat about me, which will perhaps deepen into a cloud in the midst of which I shall walk. But even now if they no longer see my outline clearly, at least they understand that I mean well by them, I am the man of the poor.

Herzl at last gets his meeting with Baron Edmond Rothschild and delivers the speech which he had prepared nearly a year before.

Paris, July 19, 1896.

Yesterday I gave the "Speech to the Rothschilds"——

I began: "A colony is a small state, a state is a large colony. You want to make a small state, I want to make a large colony."

And once again, as so many times before, I explained the whole plan. He listened to some passages with surprise, and a few times I saw admiration in his eyes.——

But he doesn't believe in the Turks.——

——After two hours of this contentious interview I picked up my umbrella and got up:

"In order to end this conversation, which we were conducting in earnest and not for our amusement, I should like to say: How shall the power of an idea be recognized? By the fact that you assume responsibility whether you say 'Yes' or 'No.'"

The Baron showed a very uncomfortable, and really very angry expression.

I elaborated: "You were the key-stone of the whole combination. If you refuse, everything I've arranged up to now will fall apart. And then I shall have to do it in another way. I shall begin a great campaign of agitation which will make it even more difficult to keep the masses under control. I wanted to give over the leadership of the whole cause to you as a philanthropic Zionist and then withdraw. Once the affair with the Sultan had been arranged you could have revealed as much and kept quiet as much as you pleased. The regulation of the mass influx is a question for the government. If, for instance, a stampede were to ensue then unfavorable reports about housing and opportunities for work might be published, which would cause the stream to slow up. These are nothing but administrative details. You consider it a misfortune to operate with such masses, but consider whether it would not be a greater misfortune if I were to set the masses in motion by means of reckless agitation.

That is just what I wanted to avoid. I have shown my good will, and that I am no headstrong intransigeant. You refuse—I have done my part."

Then I took my leave. We both declared ourselves delighted to have made each other's acquaintance, and I left.——

As Rothschild does not budge, Herzl decides: the organization of the masses must be the next step.

STARTING THE ZIONIST ORGANIZATION

——In the East End, propaganda committees are springing up spontaneously: program, the *Judenstaat*.

Party leaders: Rabbinowitz, Ish-Kishor, de Haas and others; fine, enthusiastic people.

July 20, 1896.

I wrote to de Haas in London that the organization of the masses could now begin. This will be my answer.——

BOOK FOUR

July 22, 1896, Carlsbad.

THIS MORNING I BREAKFASTED WITH NEWLINSKY IN THE hotel garden. Prince Ferdinand of Bulgaria sat down with his entourage at a table not far from us. I noticed that I was being pointed out to him. Then he sent Fürth over to tell me that he would receive me later in the garden arcade.——

I placed my idea before him in laconically short phrases. He was gripped by it swiftly.

"It is a magnificent idea," he said. "No one has ever spoken to me about the Jewish question in this fashion."

"I want to ask your Majesty to prepare the Czar for my plan and if possible to get an audience for me."

"That is difficult," he said, thoughtfully.——

He repeated that he was a friend of the Jews, and was happy to hear what I had to tell him about the Sultan and the Grand Duke of Baden.

August 23, Baden.

Long conversation with the electro-technician Kremenetzky.[11] He is a good Zionist with modern ideas. Great chemical industries might be set up around the heavily salt-laden Dead Sea.

The rivers feeding it now with sweet water would be diverted and used for drinking water. They would be

[11]John Kremenetzky, one of Herzl's first followers, head of the Jewish National Fund 1901–1907.

replaced by a canal from the Mediterranean, part of which would have to be made as a tunnel because of the mountains (a tourist spectacle), and the difference between the levels of the two seas (water-fall) could be utilized to drive machines. Many thousands of horse-power.

And even besides this there is enough water-power in Palestine which can be converted into electricity.

We must found a national Arbor Society for the reforestation of the land. Every Jew to plant one or more trees! Ten million trees!

During a conversation I had an idea about organization.

The young doctors of philosophy want to found a Zionist society of university graduates. I think it would be still better to develop Zionist professional societies for all sorts of people: societies of Jewish lawyers, physicians, technicians, engineers, building contractors, officials, merchants (chambers of commerce). In this way they are kept together by common interests. Then practical questions and plans will be laid before them, for approval, discussion, etc. If the plan is carried out then we shall have incubators for the men we need.

These professional societies shall affiliate themselves with the Zionist Organization, which will thus be aroused from its generally lamented slumbers.——

A depressing period begins now for Herzl, the work continues, but he has moments of despair. He writes to Zadoc Kahn, and asks the latter to try to win over Edmond Rothschild. A constant strain exists between Herzl and his Jewish chiefs on the Jewish-owned *Neue Freie Presse*. He seems in danger of being compelled to resign his position with the *N F P*.

In the midst of his despair he continues to work. He writes innumerable letters, and tries to reach Lord Salisbury, via Hechler.

December 1, 1896. Letter to Hechler for Lord Salisbury.

Esteemed Friend,

Your suggestion that I explain my plan about the Jews to Lord Salisbury[12] seems right to me. But I do not wish to address myself to him directly. If you think it advisable you can have him informed of the contents of this letter.

For you, my very esteemed friend, the cause of the Jews is theological. But it is also political, and very timely at that. You know that religious feelings, and recently the ubiquitous appearance of anti-Semitism, have awakened a great longing for Palestine in the broad lower masses of the Jews of all countries. You know that hundreds of thousands are prepared for immediate migration, and it is to be presumed that still more hundreds of thousands will follow them later.

This is an element—in all events a novel one—with which English policy in the Orient could and should reckon. Lord Salisbury could execute a master-stroke with this. In the present world state of affairs, dominated by the Russo-French Entente, a division of Turkey would be very disadvantageous for England. For England this division would constitute a loss, and accordingly she must desire the status quo. This can only be maintained if Turkish finances are regulated. For this reason Russia has just blocked the financial settlement suggested. Russia desires the crumbling and disintegration of Turkey.

Now there is a means of regulating Turkish finances, and with it of maintaining the *status quo* for some time longer, and simultaneously creating for England a new

[12]Lord Salisbury, British Prime Minister.

road, and the shortest one, to India. And all of this without England's laying out a penny or in any way visibly committing herself.

This means is the erection of an autonomous Jewish subject state in Palestine, similar to Egypt, under the sovereignty of the Sultan. As you know, I spun the first few threads of this when I was in Constantinople during the summer. The thing is possible if we have the support, and I expressly repeat: the invisible support of a Great Power. Since the Sultan is for the time being an unquestioned sovereign, no power can prevent him from inviting the Jews to immigrate into Palestine. For this we would procure him a substantial loan through contributions to be assured in advance and paid by the Jews.

England would be benefited by the immediate building of a railroad through Palestine from the Mediterranean to the Persian Gulf, or, in connection with the railroad the traffic will soon necessitate, through Persia and Baluchistan (and possibly Afghanistan) to India.

England would have these advantages without spending a penny, and without the world's learning of its participation. While Russia is preparing a railway line to Asia in the north, England would have a neutral reserve road to India in the south, in case difficulties were to arise around the Suez Canal.

If Lord Salisbury wishes to learn more about this idea, I am at the disposal of his minister here or of himself in London if he calls me.

If he thinks the matter too fantastic, I can only regret it. But the movement is actually in existence, and a great and adroit statesman will know how to make use of it.

With cordial greetings your obedient Theodor Herzl.

December 20, 1896.

I feel myself growing tired. I believe now more than ever before that my movement is at an end. I am fully convinced of its practicability, but I cannot overcome the initial difficulties.

A million *gulden* is all that is necessary to put the movement on its feet in a big way. This sum, so ridiculously small for so great a matter, can't be gotten, and so we shall have to go to sleep, though the day is here.

Güdemann publishes a timid attack on Herzl's ideas. Herzl replies in *Bloch's Wochenschrift*. Herzl continues his correspondence with the Grand Duke of Baden, tries to encourage his few workers. For the time being he drops the idea of a great daily, and contents himself with the publication of the weekly, *Die Welt*.

March 19, 1897.

Another conversation with Bacher. We always leave the office together now. He would like to take a trip with me to Palestine, and when I showed him the itinerary of the Maccabean Club Tour arranged by Cook he told me an old Prague legend he had heard in his youth.

"A Jewish woman was once sitting in her room looking out of the window, when she saw a black cat on the roof opposite her in labor pains. She went over, fetched the cat and helped it in its travail. Then she made a little nest of straw for the cat and the kittens in the coal bucket. A couple of days later the cat, now well again, disappeared. But the coals on which it had lain had turned into pure gold. The woman showed it to her husband, who thought that the cat had been sent by God. Accordingly he used the gold to build a temple, the Altneu Synagogue. That is how this famous building was erected.

But the man still had one wish: as a pious Jew he wanted to die in Jerusalem. And he would also have liked to see the cat again, because he wished to thank it for their prosperity. Once the woman was looking out of the window again and saw the cat on the same spot. So she called out quickly to her husband: Look, there's our cat again. The husband ran out to fetch the cat, but it leaped up and ran into the Altneu Synagogue. The husband hurried after and suddenly saw the cat sinking into the ground in the temple. There was an opening there, as into a cellar. Without thinking the husband went down through it and came to a long corridor. The cat kept on luring him further and further till finally he saw daylight again in front of him. But when he came out he was in a strange place, and the people told him he was in Jerusalem. And so he died of joy."

This story, says Bacher, proves that national consciousness had maintained itself among Jews. It really lies below the threshold of consciousness—and shimmers through; with him as well. He says he told it to me because he has also discovered a wish to go to Palestine within himself.——

Herzl begins to think of the first Congress. Munich was proposed. Now he runs up against the organized opposition of the Choveve Zion, who refused to participate in the Congress.

April 14, 1897. *From a letter to Colonel Goldsmid.*

Thank you for the cordial tone of your letter. I also am honestly in your debt and only regret that you do not understand me.

The Munich Congress is a matter that has been decided and which I can no longer retreat from. But it is also a necessity. Have Reverend Gaster show you the letter in which I recommended that the I.C.A. undertake a land-purchase which is possible now with an authorization of immigration. My suggestion, according to what Zadoc Kahn writes me, was set aside *ad acta*. These gentlemen neither wish to nor will do anything.——

The Sultan and his advisors are acquainted with the Jewish project. I spoke quite frankly to the Turkish statesmen, and they did not take it in bad part. They do not wish to give us Palestine as an independent state at any price; as a subject state (perhaps like Egypt) we might have the land of our fathers in a very short time. We might even have had it today, if my London and Paris proposals of last July had been agreed to. Do you understand my anger and impatience?

You, Colonel, should have entered Turkish service, like Woods, Kamphoevener, Goltz, and other foreign officers, as a general, and as such you would have been in command in Palestine under the sovereignty of the Sultan. Then Palestine would have fallen either to us or to our children as an independent state after the disintegration of Turkey. Was the plan so foolish? The financial arrangement would have been even simpler if the money magnates had come into it as I suggested. Montague approved my project for a loan.

Since it has not gone that way it must go another. I believe you are mistaken in not expecting any money from the masses. Each one need make only a small sacrifice, and the total achievement will be great. That will be the business of the world propaganda which will have the Munich Congress as its starting point. This, as a money matter, will be no concern of mine. There will be professional financiers in Munich who will attend to this part of the task.

In Munich after so many centuries a Jewish National Assembly is again to take place!

Is not this something so great that every Jewish heart must beat faster at the thought? Still in exile today, *leshono haboho* perhaps we shall be in the ancient home-land?

You, Colonel Goldsmid, who moved me so profoundly in Cardiff on that evening when you told me your story and began with the words: "I am Daniel Deronda"— have you no desire to take part in this Jewish National Assembly? I might understand it if you had to consider your personal position in the service, but from a Zionist standpoint you really cannot have anything against it.——

Let me be put to the test. I propose the following once more: Join with Edm. Rothschild, Montague, and whom-ever else you wish. Give me your word of honor that you will bring to a conclusion what I began in Con-stantinople—and I give you my word of honor that I will withdraw permanently from the leadership of the Jewish cause.——

May 23, 1897.

The movement is beginning in America.

Michael Singer, publisher of a new weekly, *Tolerance,* sends me reports of meetings in New York, etc.

A Rabbinical conference, with Dr. Gottheil[13] at the head, has declared itself with us.

May 10th the *New York Sun* had an article on Zionism.

[13]Dr. Richard Gottheil, Prof. at Columbia University, first President of the American Zionist Organization.

May 26, 1897.

I am working like a madman at the make-up of *Die Welt*. My closest party associates believe it is a failure.

BOOK FIVE

Opposition to the holding of the Congress in Munich is voiced by Jews in that city. Herzl is preparing to change the place to Zurich, and later makes it Basle.

June 24, 1897.

YESTERDAY, AS I WENT DOWN ON MY BICYCLE TO THE *Neue Freie Presse,* I said to myself: This is probably the last time that I am going to the *Neue Freie Presse,* for which I have taken so much trouble during so many years.

And strangely, at this thought of leaving the much envied position which I hold, recognized as the first literary position in Vienna, I felt a sort of relief—like that of the valedictorian at school.

I thought further: that is how death must be. The pain —more psychic than physical—is only in the agony. Death itself must be a sort of release to the sufferer.

Anti-Semitic attacks are made on the *N F P* because of Herzl's Zionism. Benedict alternately threatens and pleads. The break does not come. Herzl asks for a holiday to think things over.

THE FIRST CONGRESS

August 23, 1897.

Once more on the train, this time on my way to Basle, to the first Zionist Congress. The work, during these last few months, was terrific.

We shall see what the Congress will bring forth.——

One of the curiosities of this Congress will be the coming together of the various threads which I have been spinning till now. Hechler is here; Newlinsky will be here and *tutti quanti* who under my direction are helping to make this movement. It will be one of my tasks not to let them become too aware of each other, for they will lose some of their faith in me and in the ideal if they observe with what slender means I have constructed the movement up to this point. The whole thing is a marvel of equilibrium, which afterwards looks just as obvious as it looked improbable before.

One of my cares is Newlinsky: what he will say of my people, just as much as what my people will say of him. I must think up a method of keeping him out of the way.——

Here Herzl makes a partial list of the worries he has on his mind in connection with the Congress. He calls it a blindfold egg-dance.

1. The egg of the *NFP*, which I must not compromise and which I must not supply with an excuse to throw me out.
2. Egg of the Orthodox Jews.
3. Egg of the modernist Jew.
4. Egg of Austrian patriotism.
5. Egg of Turkey and Sultan.
6. Egg of the Russian government, against which nothing offensive must be said, even though the deplorable condition of the Russian Jews must be mentioned.
7. Egg of the Christian sects with regard to the Holy Places.
8. Egg of Edmond Rothschild.
9. Egg of Choveve Zion (Lovers of Zion) in Russia.

10. Egg of the colonists, who need the aid of Roth-schild, which must not be spoiled for them *tout en-considerant leurs misères*.

11. Egg of envy and jealousy. I must direct the things impersonally, yet I dare not let the reins out of my hands. It is, without exaggeration, a Hercules, for which I have no more inclination.

IMPRESSIONS OF THE FIRST CONGRESS

Vienna, September 3, 1897.

The last few days, the most important since the birth of the idea that day in Paris, have rushed by. In Basle and on the return journey I was too exhausted to make any entries, though these are more important than ever now, for others, too, have begun to note that our move-ment has entered the pages of history.

If I were to sum up the Basle Congress in one word— which I shall not do openly—it would be this: at Basle I founded the Jewish State.

If I were to say this to-day, I would be met by uni-versal laughter. In five years, perhaps, and certainly in fifty, everyone will see it. A State is founded essentially on the people for the State; yes, even on the will of one individual if he is powerful enough (the "l'Etat c'est moi" of Louis XIV). Territory is only the concrete manifesta-tion: and even where it possesses a territory, the State is always something abstract. The Church State, too, exists without a territory, or else the Pope would not be sovereign.

In Basle I created this thing which is abstract and which is therefore invisible to the great majority of

people. Actually with infinitesimal means. I gradually
infused into people the mood of the State and inspired
them with the feeling that they were the National
Assembly.

——And the Congress was splendid. Once, while Nordau was in the chair, I went to the back of the hall. The
long green table on the platform, the raised seats of the
President, the green-draped tribune, the stenographer's
and journalist's table made so powerful an impression on
me that I went out quickly, in order not to be overcome.

From an interview with the Grand Duke,
September 4, 1897.

The Grand Duke told me that he had given a detailed
report on the Zionist movement to the Kaiser. Thereupon the Kaiser had commissioned Count Eulenburg to
study the matter more closely and report on it.

The Grand Duke then told me how good relations
were between the Sultan and the Kaiser. This excellent
relationship had begun in the five year Crete affair. The
friendly service Germany had done the Turks by with-
drawing troops from Crete had made the deepest impression. German influence in Yildiz[14] was now unlimited.
England was completely shut out, to say nothing of the
other powers. And the Grand Duke added with smiling
satisfaction: "We've achieved all this without a fleet and
without making a show of anything in particular. Germany's wishes are unconditionally taken into considera-
tion. And if our Kaiser says anything to the Sultan it will
certainly be taken to heart. The only thing is that we

[14]Yildiz Kiosk, the Sultan's Palace.

must be very careful. Single steps often take a long time in world history. One must be patient. You must wait first of all for the Kaiser's return. If he received you before it might be more likely to injure the cause. You know the comments aroused everywhere by the Kaiser's trip. Well, the so-called Palestine pilgrimage, which originally was only to be of a religious nature, has now become political. This is even indicated by the Kaiser's traveling to Constantinople first, whereas originally he wanted to go direct to Palestine. So first of all he is paying the owner of the land a visit. From Palestine he is going to Egypt, that is, to another subject state of the Sultan's."

I observed that it would be very desirable if I could give the Kaiser some information before his departure, so that he could speak about Zionism in Yildiz and know what he was talking about.

The Grand Duke asked: "Are you aiming at the foundation of a state? I think that would be the only correct thing for you to do if you wish to have legal security." I had told him that before, by saying that we had no desire to subject ourselves to the accidents of a Pasha economy. "A way might be discovered of retaining the sovereign dignity of the Sultan, somewhat as in the old Danube principalities. As for what may happen later," (he smiled) "say in a generation, well, we can't know anything about that."

I then explained my often reiterated opinions, our attitude toward the insurrectionary parties, which obviously pleased him. Parbleu! I should think so!

When I mentioned what consequences Zionism had had in Russia, how socialists and anarchists are converted to Zionism, because we've given them an ideal, he nodded vigorously and said: "Pobiodonestzeff[15] ought to know that. You must tell him."——

Herzl finds difficulty in working with the Actions Committee elected by the Congress.

September 24, 1897.

I asked the gentlemen of the Actions Committee to raise some money for our work. Until now I have simply supplied the funds which were needed out of my own pocket. If the Committee wants to share in the direction of things, it must go through this test—provide five thousand *gulden* for the treasury.

Kokesch[16] declares this to be plainly impossible: *quod erat demonstrandum.* He is a very fine fellow; but where would the movement be if we depended on him?

Herzl now works on the question of the Bank. He considers this the absolute essential, now that the movement has been launched.

October 6, 1897.

I now attack the question of the Jewish Company.

The Basle Congress represents the creation of the Society of Jews for the Jewish State, even if executed weakly and with opportunistic modifications. The work of the next few years will be the creation of the Jewish Company, temporarily called the Jewish Colonial Bank.

[15]Konstantin Petrowitch Pobiodonestzeff, Russian Minister of Justice, infamous anti-Semite who is responsible for the following utterances: "There is only one way to solve the Jewish question: evacuate one third, convert a third to Christianity, and persecute the remaining third."

[16]Dr. S. Kokesch, a member of the Actions Committee.

October 27, 1897.

Dr. Mandelstamm[17] of Kiev is trying to persuade a couple of millionaires of his city to provide the money for the founding of a newspaper company. A million is needed. My father and I will contribute one hundred thousand if the Russians will get the other nine hundred thousand.

On Mandelstamm's advice I am sending a confidential agent, York Heinrich Steiner, to Kiev.

Steiner was bargaining: he wanted to have equal power with me in the paper. This I refused categorically. If anything comes of it, he will be chief administrator.

But I am so tired that I no longer care whether the newspaper is created or not. I have been too prodigal of my reserves of energy.

If the Russians supply money enough, we could perhaps even force the *Neue Freie Presse* to capitulate. With three million I could buy it out, and that would certainly be the best thing. With the *Neue Freie Presse* in our hand we could work wonders.

November 29, 1897.

Nordau writes he is making efforts to be received by the German Kaiser for Zionist purposes. If he succeeds, he will be the foremost person in the movement which I have created. But I find this the right thing. The work must grow beyond me. I write him my consent and ask him to go also to Pobiodonestzeff and the Czar. I am also writing him that I wish to make him Governor of the

[17]Dr. Max Mandelstamm, Ducent of the University of Kiev, one of the first Russian Zionists.

Jewish Bank. Jealousy is stupid, and I am not "on the make." My present dream is: to write a drama in verse (costumes of the time of the Renaissance).

Wolffsohn, Kahn and others are at work on the Bank, while Herzl continues his negotiations leading ultimately to the interview with the Kaiser. The Zionist movement has been launched, but it is penniless.

March 26, 1898.

I am still fighting with a wooden sword, like a clown, or like a child.

I need a sword of steel—i.e., a great newspaper, with which to carry on political activities, render services to people, make connections, etc.

So I struggle helplessly and cannot move forward. It is horrible to have such clear plans, to see the road so plainly, and to be condemned to impotence. I need a miserable million in order to direct a great newspaper, and for this service to the Jewish people I cannot get the help. For two years the thing has been so . . .

Fructus percipiendi! The lost opportunities of Zionism.

His own money is being eaten up by *Die Welt,* which has less than three thousand circulation.

May 5, 1898.

Die Welt keeps eating up money, and I must make it self-supporting, or it will go under. I can keep it going for perhaps another year without ruining myself.

Die Welt gets no help from the party; yes, there is even talk of a Yiddish paper to be subventioned by the

Committee, which would to some extent compete with
Die Welt.

The dreams of the Bank dwindle. At first Herzl thinks of a
minimum of sixty million *francs*. But when the efforts to interest
wealthy Jews seem to be hopeless, Herzl has to fall back on the
idea of launching the Bank through the Congress.

August 9, 1898.

Wolffsohn reports that only one hundred thousand
pounds have been raised for the Bank.

Everything depends on whether a decent increase
can be made on this sum in the few weeks before the
Congress.

If not, then the enthusiasms of the Congress must on
this occasion be exploited for the Bank. A tremendously
difficult task. The rich fellows want to freeze us out.

August 11, 1898.

Friedrich S. was here, from Paris. I reminded him of
the opinion he expressed three years ago when I read
him the manuscript of the *Judenstaat* in the Hotel Castille,
Rue Cambon. He was ashamed, pained, and said: "I have
been converted. You really were right."

It was the Dreyfus affair which converted him.

And like this man, who considered me a lunatic, so the
others, who still consider me one, will also come round.

But how would it have been if I had let myself be dis-
suaded by this man? The world would have been poorer
by an idea, and the Jewish people by a great movement.

How big is the responsibility which these people bear
who tried to prevent me from going ahead, and how light
is the punishment which they must suffer.

He is uncomfortable for a moment, and says: "You are right!"

The Second Congress passed by with little notice in the *Diaries*.

THE SECOND CONGRESS

August 29, 1898.

——In the afternoon there was the financial report. And then stupidities began. Gaster presided with a heavy hand. To my utter despair[18] Oskar Marmorek praised the Actions Committee because it had achieved so much with such small means! And there in the gallery sat Newlinsky, whom I had invited with wife and child in order that he might report to the Sultan how powerful our movement had become! Then Bernstein-Kohan[19] took the floor and praised us because we had been able to do this without any money. I sent word to him to shut up, or I would leave the Congress. He continued to talk stupidly, and spoke again and again of our poverty—until I broke up the session to let the finance committee meet.

And these are the instruments with which I must work. They break in my hand, as the wooden papercutter broke during the stormy session.——

In September Herzl sees Bülow,[20] Hohenlohe,[21] Eulenburg[22] and the Grand Duke of Baden. The idea has already come to him of

[18]Oskar Marmorek, architect, a member of the El Arish delegation.

[19]Dr. Jacob Bernstein-Kohan, a member of the Actions Committee, one of the Russian Zionist leaders.

[20]Graf von Bülow, German Foreign Minister.

[21]Hohenlohe, German Prime Minister.

[22]Eulenburg, German Ambassador to Vienna.

a temporary territory—with Palestine as the ultimate goal. So he writes in July:

I am thinking of giving the movement a nearer territorial goal, with Zion as the final objective.

The poor masses need immediate help.

Perhaps we can get Cyprus from England—and even bear South Africa and America in mind.

The Hague, September 30, 1898.

Traveled again through the sweet-smelling landscape of Holland. But not as I did the first time. Then, in 1885, I was a young dreamer, void of content, seeing only the form of things.

To-day the land says something else to me.

I see a city rise suddenly out of the plain, without hill, river, or sea—without any encouragement, so to speak. That is the Hague.

A proof that the will makes the city.

If I point with my finger to a certain place and say: Let a city rise here—then a city rises.

The whole of Holland is proof of what man can create on the most thankless soil.

When a young man is in love he sees his beloved under every bonnet.

So everything I see reminds me of my idea.

BOOK SIX

October 14, 1898.

THE PARTING FROM MY DEAR ONES WAS VERY PAINFUL THIS
time. I could remain peacefully in my beautiful home,
with my lovely children, whose rosy childhood years are
passing without my being able to enjoy them. They are
growing up and I am not there to observe in detail the
charm of their development.

October 1st Herzl received a letter from Prince Eulenburg
advising him that the German Kaiser expects to receive him in
Palestine. But he has to worry lest the new leave of absence
which he must take from the *Neue Freie Presse* will cost him his
position. Herzl manages to adjust his difficulties with the *Neue
Freie Presse,* and on October 18 is received by the German Kaiser
in Constantinople.

October 19, 1898.

The Kaiser, in the dark uniform of a Hussar, came
toward me. I stood still and made a deep bow. He came
up to me, almost to the door, and offered me his hand. I
believe he said that he was glad to see me, or something
like that.

I said: "Your Imperial Majesty, I am happy to be the
recipient of this distinction."

Then he went back round the table, pushed an arm-
chair toward me, waved his hand in a gesture of invitation and sat down with his back to the table: he crossed
his legs, which were encased in Hussar's boots, like one

who is settling comfortably for a long talk. Von Bülow had entered behind me, and sat down at the same time as I. Like myself he held his top hat all the time on his knees. I had forgotten to remove the glove of my right hand, according to the rules of etiquette.——

I had expected that he would begin volubly and therefore I was somewhat out of breath when he bade me speak.

"Where shall I begin, your Imperial Majesty?"

"Where you will," he said somewhat ironically, and leaned back.

I repeated the contents of my letter of the day before: my voice shook somewhat, and my heart beat violently against my ribs. And I was angry that Bülow, who is not favorably disposed toward me, should see my embarrassment and certainly be delighted by it. But for all that I said nothing foolish. My fear was only in my voice. But when I came to the question of the Land Company and the German Protectorate, he nodded rapidly and contentedly, as his habit is, more with his eyes than with his head. It is a highly characteristic movement. He looks sharply and powerfully at you—the Kaiser!—and when he is pleased by an observation or phrase, his lips are pressed together and his splendid eyes say: "I understand you— you are my man—first class."

He soon took over the lead and explained why he considered the Zionist movement of worth. Unfortunately I was an embarrassed listener, and I had to exert all my strength in preparing the replies, so that I have not been able to retain all the details. He never mentioned the Jews except as my "*Landsleute*"—and not in an exactly friendly tone. He had no doubt that we had sufficient money and man-power at our disposal to carry out the colonization of Palestine. Here my attention failed a little, for I could not help noting that my three years of work have made of the word "Zionism" a familiar term which the Kaiser used freely in speaking with me.

"There are," he said, "among your *Landsleute* certain elements which it would be well to have immigrate into Palestine. I am thinking, for instance, of those cases where there are a number of usurers among the country people. If these were to take their wealth and settle in the colonies, they would make themselves more useful." Those were his words, more or less.

I was angered that he should identify the Jews with a few usurers, and in my indignation I suddenly found myself cool and controlled again, and I made a short speech against anti-Semitism, which had stabbed us to the heart. We had been deeply pained. . . .

The Kaiser observed that he believed the Jews would set about the colonization of Palestine if they knew that he would keep them under his protection, and that they really would not be leaving Germany.

Bülow supplemented with: "And they will, we hope, be grateful for it." But he drew my attention to the fact that the rich Jews did not agree with my idea. "The big papers, too, are not for it, and your own amongst them. You ought to think of getting one or the other of the big papers on your side."

I said: "Your excellency, that is purely a matter of money. As a writer I regret to have to say it."

Bülow's intentions were quite clear. He wanted to let the Kaiser understand that I had no power behind me.

Bülow said whatever he could in opposition to me, without using the word "No," which he dared not do, for the *voluntas regis* was obviously "Yes." He kept saying: "Yes, yes—Yes, but—Yes, if only—"; nothing but masked negatives.

I felt my arguments growing stronger and stronger under the encouragement of the Kaiser's approval.

I soon touched on the subject of the opportune moment that lay before Germany, what with France's inner weakness——

The conversation lagged for a moment after the French chapter. I made use of the pause to come back to the subject.

"And for that reason France cannot raise any objections to our aim." For Russia, too, it would be a solution, etc.—all the usual arguments.

The Kaiser then said with a touch of humor which had more joviality then heartlessness in it: "Yes, your *Landsleute* haven't had such a good time of it in Russia these last couple of hundred years."

I went on, and while he nodded approval unfolded the whole subject before him. I think I laid down all the arguments: Russia's Siberian railroad line, which might prove for Europe a Pandora's box of immeasurable evils. Everything, everything. He listened splendidly, at times; and when I touched on the complicated forms of the loan we could make for Turkey, with evident effort and tension. I said, finally: "I don't know whether it is because I am so gripped by the subject—but the whole thing appears quite natural to me."

He looked at me powerfully: "To me, too."

First Contact With Palestine

October 27, 1898. Written in Rishon le Zion.

The last two nights which we spent on the little ship *Russia*—coming here from Alexandria—were intolerably hot; the five of us were in one cabin. At three in the morning I was already out on the deck.——

In Jaffa

The landing began uncomfortably—Jaffa.

Again poverty and desolation and heat, in brilliant colors.

We straggled through the streets to the hotel, as no carriage was obtainable. I was already on horseback, setting out of Rishon, when Dr. Jaffa[23] managed to get a carriage for me.

We went first—in a fearful heat—to Mikveh Israel. It is a splendid agricultural school. Flags and ornaments decorated the gate in honor of the Kaiser, who will be passing this way to-morrow on the road to Jerusalem. I shall try to persuade him to visit this institution.

From Mikveh, through the landscape made desolate by Arab neglect, toward the much-praised Rishon le Zion. For a poor village it is not so badly off. But any one who expects more than a poor settlement is doomed to disappointment. Deep dust on roads, a little green.——

The colonists showed us the wine-cellers, ceremoniously. But I have never doubted that money can build industrial establishments anywhere.

[23]Dr. Hillel Jaffa, representative of the Russian "Lovers of Zion" in Palestine, a member of Herzl's Committee to El Arish.

On October 28, the famous scene takes place outside Mikveh Israel—the reception of Herzl by the German Kaiser, in sight of the colonists.

October 29, 1898, Jerusalem.

We rode forth, the day before yesterday, from Rishon le Zion. At a distance of half an hour is the Jewish village of Vaad el Chanin. There the entire population turned out to meet us, children singing; an old man greeted us with bread and salt and wine from his own soil. I had to visit almost every house in the colony.

We rode. A cavalcade came storming out to meet us from Rehoboth, some twenty young fellows who staged a sort of fantasia, sang Hebrew songs, and swarmed around our carriage. Wolffsohn, Schnirer,[24] Bodenheimer[25] and I had tears in our eyes, as we saw these swift, manly riders into whom our pants-selling boys can be transformed. I was reminded of the Far West riders of the American plains, whom I once saw in Paris.

At nine o'clock movement on the road, which was covered with a mixed multitude of Arab beggars, women, children and horsemen, indicated the approach of the Imperial party. Grim looking Turkish horsemen came riding first, with reins loose, with threatening weapons and still more threatening looks. Then the outriders. And then last a gray group, with some ladies, and with the Kaiser himself.

[24] Dr. M. Schnirer, one of the founders of the Kadimah Club in Vienna, member of the delegation which appeared with Herzl, before King Wilhelm II of Germany.

[25] Dr. Max Bodenheimer, a member of Herzl's delegation to meet the German Kaiser in Palestine; head of the Jewish National Fund 1907-1914.

I gave the sign to the school choir of Mikveh to sing the *Heil Dir im Siegerkranz*. I took my place by the side of one of the ploughs, and took off my sun helmet. The Kaiser recognized me from a distance. He started slightly, reined in his horse toward me—and stopped opposite me. I stepped forward two paces; and as he bent over his horse's neck and stretched out his hand to me, I came quite close to him and stretched out mine, and remained standing with bared head.

He laughed, and flashed with his kingly eyes:

"How are you?"

"I thank Your Majesty. I am seeing the country. How has Your Majesty's journey been so far?"

His eyes flashed.

"Very hot. But the land has a future."

"At present it is still sick," I said.

"It needs water, much water," he said, speaking downward at me.

"Yes, Your Majesty. Colonization on a grand scale."

He repeated: "It is a land of the future."

Perhaps he said something more which I have now forgotten, for the interview lasted several minutes. Then he stretched his hand out to me again and galloped off. The Kaiserin had also ridden forward a little, and nodded to me, smiling. Then, while the childish voices sang the *Heil Dir im Siegerkranz*, the Imperial suite moved forward.

Among the horsemen I recognized the Court Marshal, Eulenburg, who greeted me in all friendliness.

The spectators of Mikveh Israel were utterly dazed. A few of them asked who that had been. The Rothschild administrators looked timid and irritated.

Wolffsohn, the fine fellow, had taken two snapshots. At least, so he thought. He tapped his kodak proudly. "I wouldn't give up this film for ten thousand marks."

But when we got to the photographer in Jaffa and had the plates developed, we saw that one of the snapshots showed the shadow of the Kaiser and my left foot, while the other was completely spoiled.

October 31, *Jerusalem.*

When I remember thee in time to come, O Jerusalem, it will not be with delight.

The dreary deposits of two thousand years filled with inhumanity, intolerance and filth lie in your evil-smelling alleys. The only human being always here, the sweet dreamer of Nazareth, did nothing but help increase the hate.

If Jerusalem is ever ours, and if I can still accomplish anything at that time, the first thing I'd do would be to clean it up.

I would clear out everything that's not holy, set up workers' quarters outside the city, clean out and tear down the nests of filth, burn the ruins which aren't holy, and set the bazaars down somewhere else. Then, retaining as much of the old style of architecture as possible, I would build a comfortable, airy, properly drained new city around the holy places.

This afternoon we were on the Mount of Olives.

Great moments. What could not be made out of this landscape. A city like Rome, and the Mount of Olives would give a view like the Gianicolo.

I would seal up the old city with its relics, remove the daily traffic, and leave only houses of worship and welfare institutions within the old wall. And on the hilly slopes round about, which our labors would make green, a magnificent New Jerusalem would rise. The most elegant people from every part of the world would travel on the road to the Mount of Olives. A jewel can be made of Jerusalem through care. Everything holy to be shut up in the old walls, everything new to be spread around outside.

We climbed the Russian Tower, I only to the first gallery, because I got dizzy, the others all the way up. Incomparable view of the Jordan Valley with its mountainous slopes, the Dead Sea, the Mountains of Moab, the eternal city Jerusalem.

November 2, 1898.

Eight minutes past one.

We are back from the audience.

This short reception will be remembered forever in Jewish history, and it is not impossible that it will have historic consequences.

But how bald the details of the whole procedure are.——

We drove in the blazing noon-day sun and white dust to the tents. A couple of Jews in the streets looked up as we drove by. Geese in the swamp starting up at the wild geese flying above. At the entrance to the tent the Turkish guard hesitated before it let us pass.——

Then they called us in to the Kaiser's tent.

——The four men entered the broad tent, after me. I asked whether I might introduce the gentlemen and the

Kaiser nodded. As every name was called off, he raised his hand to the tip of his helmet.——

When I finished he said the following, more or less.

"I thank you for your communications, which have interested me greatly. The matter must in any case be studied more closely and discussed at greater length."—— "The land must have water and shade above everything else." He made use of a number of technical agricultural and forestry terms. He had learned, he said, that the soil was cultivable.

"The settlements which I have seen, the German as well as those of your *Landsleute*, may serve as a model of what can be done in this country. The land has room for all. Only provide water and shade. For the native population, too, the colonies can serve as models to be imitated. Your movement, with which I am well acquainted, contains a healthy idea."——

As soon as his official reply was over, he stretched out his hand to me, but did not let us go yet. He drew us into conversation together with Bülow.

"You know Herr von Bülow, don't you?"

Did I know him! Bülow, who had followed with his finger the copy of the document which I had read forth, smiled sweetly. We spoke about the journey.

The Kaiser said: "We happen to have struck the hottest weather. At Ramleh the temperature was thirty-one in the shade and forty-one in the sun."

Bülow said sweetly: "As Your Majesty was gracious enough to say, the weather is the most important thing. Herr Herzl knows better than I what the Greek poet says: Αριστον μέν ύδωρ.

"That we can bring into the country. It will cost billions but it will bring billions in return."

"Well, you certainly don't lack the money," exclaimed the Kaiser jovially, and slapped his whip against his boots. "You have more money than all the rest of us."

Bülow expatiated on this point. "Yes, yes. Money, which makes so much difficulty for us, you have abundantly."

At this point I remarked how the water power of the Jordan could be used, and drew Seidener, as an engineer, into the conversation. Seidener spoke about dams, etc. The Kaiser entered readily into the discussion, and carried the idea further. Then he mentioned the health question, eye diseases, etc., which spread particularly during the fig harvest season. Then I drew Schnirer into the conversation, and he spoke briefly on this subject.

On his return to Europe Herzl finds that his audiences with the Kaiser have had a very "poor press." Herzl was certain that enemies had been at pains to minimize his work.

November 15, 1898.

The intended journey to Rome must also be given up for the moment. In Naples I got news from Newlinsky: he writes he is sick and cannot make the journey.

I believe this is only an excuse.

December 20, 1898.

The founding of the Bank drags along in the face of ludicrous difficulties. Wolffsohn reports that he has carried through the formal founding.

January 16, 1899.

We are stuck. Something must happen. I have decided to try to get an audience from the Czar through Baroness von Suttner.

February 11, 1899.

Days of discouragement. The tempo of the movement is slowing up. Our slogans are getting used up. Our ideas have become oratorical effects, and the effects are becoming dull.

I am afraid to face the question of the Bank subscriptions. Wolffsohn reports that no reputable bank will accept subscriptions. Kahn[26] had the curious idea of using Cook's[27] offices as subscription centers. I shall veto that.

Hechler wants to go to Karlsruhe again. The Grand Duke telegraphed him he could come. I shall give him instructions to take along.

He goes to see the Grand Duke, and finds him favorably inclined, but will not act without the consent of the Kaiser. Herzl feels he must get another audience from the Kaiser. The latter refers him to Bülow. Herzl writes to Bülow, the Grand Duke and others—but things do not move. Above all the Bank worries him.

March 29, 1899.

This morning I got a wire from the Colonial Bank which thoroughly depressed me.

The results of the first day's subscriptions are—8,000 shares.——

I am now in the mood in which Faust was when he

---

[26]Jacobus Kahn, Dutch banker, one of Herzl's first followers.
[27]Cook's Travel Agency.

was ready to sell his soul to the devil under any pact. If any man were to promise me the success of the shares to-day, I would sell him ten years of my life.

April 21, 1899.

The incompetence of the London bank office surpasses all bounds. Is it unwillingness or laziness? To-day, during the last week of the subscription, we receive the figures for the Russian subscription to go into *Die Welt*—which appeared yesterday! The Rumanian figures are not here.

I shall go to Cologne to-morrow to discuss things. I had still wanted to finish this sixth volume of the Diaries with a definite chapter—the success or the failure of the subscriptions.

As it is the book ends with a big

?

BOOK SEVEN

April 25, 1899.

NEVER WAS A GREATER TASK UNDERTAKEN WITH MORE INADE-quate means.

To-morrow I must again ask pardon of my "chiefs" for the leave of absence I have taken without their permission. Who knows how long they will let me carry on this way?

The movement demands my constant travel; and there is no doubt about it that the *Neue Freie Presse* can dismiss me for neglect of duty "with all the respect in the world for differences of opinion." This pitiful clash of duties wearies me, unnerves me and wears me out more than anything else.

Hague, June 13, 1899.

At the World Peace Conference.

If I were younger, the movement these days in the Hague would give me plenty of material for these books. But I am used up, blasé, with all these struggles and adventures.

This explains the fact that people who do and experience many wonderful things seldom write anything wonderful.

I came here because the Baroness von Suttner is here and might bring me together with some of the Czar's people.

Immediately on the first evening I became acquainted with the Russian Senator Bloch,[28] who gave the Czar this peace idea. A clever, educated old merchant Jew. He interests me and, it appears, I him.

Paris, June 19, 1899, *in the Hotel Castille.*

Out of a feeling of piety I still stay, when in Paris, in this old place where I wrote my *Judenstaat* four years ago. What a time it has been since then! And what exhaustion. My heart is used up. I suffer from heart pains, arrhythmia.

August 11, 1899. (*on the way to the Third Congress*)

During these days something occupies my mind more than my still unprepared Congress speech, the Princess, and my slavery in the *Neue Freie Presse*—namely, the plan for my new drama, *Die Sündige Mutter,* which charms me in prospect.

His impressions of the Third Congress are brief.

August 21, 1899.

The Congress went off smoothly. A good atmosphere was again achieved—and that in turn will be lost gradually. But the work was made easier for us this time by an advance loan on the *shekels.* The good Schalit[29] of Riga, Dr. Katzenelson[30] and Sachs promised five thousand

---

[28]Bloch, Russian Diplomat (of Jewish ancestry).
[29]Schalit, a rich merchant of Riga, a Russian Zionist leader.
[30]Dr. Katzenelson, of Libau, a Russian Zionist leader.

kronen each, so that I could take steps toward Turkey and promise N. . . . direct *baksheesh* (graft).

And now, after having for a week tasted what it feels like to be free and a master, I must go back to my wretched slavery on the *Neue Freie Presse*, where I am not allowed to have an opinion of my own. And the question is that of a miserable few thousand gulden which I dare not, as the father of a family, give up.

August 29, 1899.

My work will look much more marvelous when people will get to know with what money worries I had to struggle as a result of efforts for Zionism.

On August 28th, Herzl goes to see N. Bey in person, in Vienna. Herzl also renews his efforts to reach the Russian Czar while working on Turkish statesmen.

August 30, 1899.

To-day, as I sat on the rattling omnibus which took me out to Währing, I thought of my Zion novel, *Altneuland*.

I got the hint from the name of the Prague *Altneuschul*. It will become a famous word.

December 29, 1899.

Yesterday I had a talk with the American Ambassador to Turkey, Oscar Straus, who was passing through Vienna.

A man of middle height, lean, thin reddish beard, hook-nosed, Jewish protruding ears, thin hair, dry, smart, and yet sympathetic because of his honest eyes. After five minutes we were on intimate terms, although he said in advance that I had the reputation of being indiscreet. But he did not take my disregard of consequences in bad part, for in such big things one could not spare persons. He himself, as a man in office, could be neither for nor against Zionism. He considered my word of honor, that I would say nothing in the open about our interview, as superfluous.——

Straus is for Mesopotamia! He knew that quite a time ago a pamphlet on Mesopotamia, by Cyrus Adler,[31] was sent to me through certain friends in America (Richard Sulzberger and others).

Bank problems, problems of diplomatic negotiations, problems of the organization, accumulate. Meanwhile he has to appear in the office of his newspaper every day.

March 17, 1900.

With all these things in my head, I had to go to the office to-day to write a light paragraph about the Fashion Show for the *Neue Freie Presse*. Clown and leader in one. Moses had it easier.

From an interview with the Grand Duke. April 18, 1900.

——I opened the duel with a description of the situation, something like my letter of March 5.

I had been quite surprised when the amiable Grand Duke at my arrival expressly thanked me for my letter "of March 5." By chance I had read through this letter

---

[31]Dr. Cyrus Adler, Orientalist, founder of numerous cultural institutions in the U.S.A.

again that morning at the hotel, in order to prepare myself for the interview, so that I knew what he was speaking about. I also made mention of the Paris exposition and the consequent pacifist feeling on the part of France, under the influence of the considerations which seemed to me to make the present moment suitable for a campaign in Constantinople.

I had given a brief and compressed sketch of the situation, after which the Grand Duke began to speak:

The matter was quite different. It was just the South African war in its present stage which was a danger for Germany, and for the peace of the world as well. The moment might come when England would see that it could not finish the Boers off. Then a pretext might be looked for to abandon the Transvaal, because "more important interests were at stake."

Probably even now England was avid for a diversion in a direction where its power was still unenfeebled and superior. It would take care not to pick a quarrel itself with Russia; France also was too strong for it on the sea. But as against that it might not be averse to throwing itself on Germany, which was still incapable of defending itself at sea but which nevertheless provided a significant point of attack through the striking growth of its commerce.——

Germany was in general retreating from complications of any sort, said the Grand Duke, and avoiding anything that might give England cause for the desired wrangle. For this reason Radolin, the Ambassador in Petersburg, of whose recall there had been rumors, had been elevated, solely that he might remain there. For this reason the invalid ambassador in London had not been replaced; for this reason the old man Muenster was remaining in Paris, only for *quieta non movere*.

Germany feels itself unusually menaced by England's defeats in South Africa. I should never have drawn this conclusion from the situation.——

I must admit that the German argument put forth by the Grand Duke has something in it.

Germany's exposure on the sea is enormous, and her capacity for defense, as the Grand Duke says, very small. "We would not be capable of defending ourselves against a blockade. 15 years will go by before our fleet is finished. But our commerce and our industry are expanding day by day, in a way which is just as pleasing as disquieting."——

In England there was in any case great dissatisfaction with the progress made by German industry and world commerce. They would be glad to pull us to pieces. France and Russia could only encourage that. And if our industry, our overseas commerce and merchant marine, were ruined that might suit the English very well.

This danger of a war on the sea, with its possibilities of economic ruin and the deprivation of so many people of bread, was one of the greatest concerns of the German government. In spite of the German land power such a danger was possible, and perhaps the only combination that might give promise of a certain security was America.

But in any case the greatest caution was imperative, and it was impossible to be subjected to the eventuality of England's making a German protectorate in Palestine a pretext for turning its attention from South Africa to "this more important question."

But a ray of light in this situation was the imminent visit of the Kaiser Franz Josef to Berlin.——

"But to return to your affair: although we are not in a position at the moment to recommend you in Constantinople, Austria certainly is. After his return from Berlin, the recommendation of the Austrian Kaiser will have much more weight than might have been the case before or even now. Both Kaisers of Central Europe now have far greater importance."——

But under no circumstances did Germany wish to expose itself, and nothing could be done by the German Ambassador.

I should have myself recommended to the Sultan by Austria. Since the Bagdad railway affair Russia had gained the upper hand in Turkey. It had been possible to make the Sultan understand that it was better not to depend on one friend (Germany), who was demanding such concessions for itself. Now Russian influence was overwhelming in Constantinople.

"When are you going to Constantinople?" he finally asked.

"I don't know yet, Your Royal Highness. I'm going to London first. I want to try to see Lord Salisbury, in case his South African troubles leave any room for anything else in his head. Perhaps I can interest him in Zionism. The purely Zionist idea, without a German protectorate, has many friends in England. That is, in the church, and they surely have social, and perhaps also political influence."

He nodded in assent.

"If I succeed in winning over Lord Salisbury, would it be easier to obtain German intervention in our favor, since this is the only objection which seems to cause concern?"

"Then," said the Grand Duke, "there would still be the question of persuading Count Bülow of it."——

To what extent I shall be able to use with Lord Salisbury what the Grand Duke told me I do not know at the moment. Perhaps I may be able to contrive a rapprochement between England and Germany precisely on the basis of Zionism.

April 25, 1900. *London*.

Bank worries.

In the city I am a sort of banker. Curious adventure. In the Burlington Hotel, in 1898, I was a promotor. Now the Bank is established, *aber fragt mich nur nicht wie*, but don't ask me how it was done.

May 1, 1900.

The poor Jews really have extraordinarily bad luck. When a man does arise who could and would help them— for I am convinced that by my personal intervention I have moved things forward swiftly—then he must be economically enslaved, and must tremble for his children's bread.

I have a first class epitaph for myself:

"He had too high an opinion of the Jews."

On June 2nd it is decided to hold the next Congress [the Fourth] in London, instead of in Basle. Herzl reads in the papers that the

famous traveler Arminius Vambery has been called from Budapest to the Sultan. He sees at once a new approach. He sends
Hechler to Budapest and arranges a meeting with Vambery. Herzl
is at a loss as to the next course of action.

June 11, 1900.

The difference between me and Sabbatai Zevi[32] is, apart
from the changes in the technical possibilities, this:
Sabbatai Zevi made himself great, so that he might be
the equal of the great of the earth. But I find the great
small, as small as myself.

June 17, 1900.

Yesterday I traveled fourteen hours express from
Vienna to Mühlbach to see Vambery, stayed fifteen
hours, and then hurried back because my wife is in bed
with inflammation of the throat.

I learned to know, in this limping, seventy-year-old
Hungarian Jew, one of the most interesting of men. He
does not know any more whether he is a Turk or an
Englishman. He is a German writer, speaks twelve lan-
guages with equal perfection. He told me a thousand and
one stories of the Orient, of his intimacy with the Sultan
etc.

He immediately had complete confidence in me.——
He began:

"I don't want any money; I am a rich man. I could
eat gold beefsteaks if I wanted to. I have a quarter of a
million and don't need more than half of my income. If
I help you, it is for the sake of the cause."

He listened to the details of our plan, the money ques-

[32]Sabbatai Zevi, a messianic pretender, 1626–1675.

tion, etc. He told me confidentially that the Sultan had called him in order to influence the European papers in his behalf. Could I help along?

I answered evasively.

In between he returned to the noteworthiest of his adventures, which were noteworthy enough. In Turkey he had begun his career as a singer in a coffee-house; a year and a half later he had been intimate with the Grand Vizier. He could have slept in the Yildiz Kiosk (palace) but might have been murdered. He eats at the Sultan's table—absolutely informal—but he can't get the thought of poison out of his head. And a hundred other picturesque things.

I said to him: "Vambery Bashi—if I may call you by the name Nordau uses—write to the Sultan to receive me. First, because I can serve him in the press. Second, because the mere fact of my appearing there will raise his credit.

"What I should like most would be to have you as interpreter."

But he was afraid of the strain of the summer journey. When I left it was uncertain whether he would do anything.

BOOK EIGHT

Herzl's health begins to show signs of the strain. June 21st he has an attack in the office of the Welt. With difficulty he must arrange for a three-day rest.

Herzl falls sick on the eve of the Fourth Congress, and is confined to his bed for three days.

London, August 14, 1900.

The Fourth Congress is the best attended we have had so far. Its proceedings are already in the papers.

I myself have felt no inner richness of experience from this Congress. The mass meeting on Sunday evening, in the East End, no longer meant anything to me. The cheers of the crowd mean nothing more.

A new note was the Botanical Garden party on Sunday. The entire public followed me around in compact masses. I should have liked to enjoy this fine English garden, but I was crushed under royal honors. They looked at me in amazement as I drank a cup of tea. They put out children toward me, introduced ladies to me; gray-haired old men wanted to kiss my hand. And whenever they did these things, I wanted to ask them: "Excuse me, why do you do these things?"

Yesterday, during the afternoon session, I handed the chair over to Gaster and Nordau, and hurried to Kensington Gardens. There, amid the lovely scenery, in front of the lake, I drank a cup of tea in peace.

September 20, Vienna.

Une idée qui me hante (an idea which haunts me) is the emergency insurance I wanted to launch in London and which I was prevented from doing by the opposition of the leaders.

Yesterday I brought it up in the Actions Committee again. It's the only thing we can do. A mutual Jewish emergency insurance. The insured victims of Jewish persecution will receive a minimum sum for re-settlement. It was shown in the Rumanian emigration that 200 florins per person were necessary. It could not be obtained from philanthropists. Refugees must have some legal rights. These rights must be obtained by everyone through the purchase of a policy. Cases of need may be counted from 100 to 200 gulden. Naturally the principal thing is the definition of an emergency and the prevention of fraud.

This would have to be construed on the analogy of accident insurance. The company's headquarters I imagine would be in Basle.

Greater insurance might also be taken with steeply progressive premiums.

If two florins are to be paid yearly for 200 florins, five or six would be paid for 400, and for 1000 florins not five-fold but ten-fold or more, because then a single case of damage immediately presents a series.

To my astonishment Kokesch, who is otherwise very careful and who reasons matter-of-factly, was on my side. That encouraged me very much.

An unhoped-for opportunity suddenly presents itself for a new approach to the Turkish Powers. But the affair with Turkey drags on and dies out. In between a new combination offers itself whereby Herzl may become independent of the *Neue Freie Presse*, but again this comes to nothing.

January 30, 1901.

Three months torn out of my life, in fragments, in "great expectations."

First it was that fellow C. who pulled me around, and then the big industrialists with their newspaper. In between I let my novel[33] lie unwritten, and the longer it lies unwritten the worse it becomes, and the less desire I have for it.

Now I must go again to London, and it will be three weeks before I can sit down at my writing-table.

The wind blows through the stubble. I feel my autumn coming. I run the risk of leaving for my children neither a work for the world, nor yet money.

It would be ridiculous for me to start the novel two days before I leave. But I give myself my word of honor that I shall begin it immediately on my return.

March 14, 1901.

I am working eagerly now at *Altneuland*.

My hopes of practical success have melted away. My life is no longer a romance. But the romance is now my life.

March 21.

The beginning of spring.

Yesterday was a peculiar and I think important day. Levontin, the bank director, who had come from Russia,

[33]Referring to *Altneuland*.

explained to me, Wolffsohn, Kremenetzky, Marmorek, Kokesch, his plan for buying up the shares and accessories of the Jaffa-Jerusalem railroad. I thought the idea magnificent. I may have found my long sought banking man in Levontin.[34]

I accepted this plan and am sending him today to Paris, where the Palestinian Navon lives, who is selling the railroad shares.

Next week Levontin will be here again. Then he is going to London as sub-manager of the Trust. He's staying there till the autumn to settle the affairs of the Colonial Bank. Then we are sending him to Jaffa as manager of our branch.

But outwardly it is not to be a branch, but an independent bank with its headquarters in Germany, Cologne.

I had Marmorek write to Bodenheimer yesterday that he was to prepare the statutes etc. of the bank for Jerusalem and Jaffa. Capital shares 500,000 marks with 50 per cent in deposits. The Trust will take over the shares and put them in portfolio, in order to give out the minority shares later upon the profits accruing.

The majority shares of the Jaffa Railroad as of all undertakings will always have to remain in the possession of the Trust.

Next week I'm calling Beer, who is to go to Palestine for the erection of a cement and tile factory.

The idea also flashed through my mind yesterday of buying a Mediterranean shipping company, that is, a bad one whose majority shares can be bought cheaply and

[34] Z. D. Levontin, first General Director of the Anglo-Palestine Co. in Jaffa.

which we will then clean up. The "Adria" in Fiume
would be suitable for that, as I see by a fleeting glimpse
at the stock exchange register.

Levontin also has the idea of making our Jaffa Bank
the depository for the Turkish government of the tolls
and taxes in Palestine.

For a time Herzl plays with the idea of settling in London, to
be in better position for Zionist work. Nothing comes of this plan.

May 2, 1901.

To-day I am forty-one years old:
> "The wind blows through the stubble;
> My steps must now be double."

Nearly six years have passed since I began this movement which has made me old, tired and poor.

BOOK NINE

Unexpectedly comes the call to Constantinople, a hasty meeting of the Actions Committee takes place in Herzl's house, and he issues instructions all around in the event of a successful interview with the Sultan.

Interminable worries over *baksheesh* block and hinder his progress. On May 18th he at last accomplishes what he has so long dreamed of: the interview with the Sultan, Abdul Hamid.

May 13, 1901. *Constantinople.*

HERE, AFTER FIVE YEARS, I SIT IN THE SAME ROYAL HOTEL, in the same room that I occupied when I began the business through Newlinsky. I look out of the window at the Golden Horn, as another man. Beauty no longer moves me. The world has ceased to be Imagination, and has become Will.——

May 19, 1901

Sometimes I am compelled to withhold my fresh impressions from this book, because I should have to put them down in the very place where an unlucky chance of spying trick might turn them into an accusation against me. Here, on the Rumanian ship on the Black Sea, I feel free.

That is why the favorable things which I here put down about the Sultan will have, for the future, the value of the truth.

Naturally neither his order nor his diamond have influenced me in the slightest. These things leave me, as they would every other sensible man, quite cold. For me they have only political value, which I calmly estimate, neither overvaluing nor undervaluing it. I believe that we can make some sort of capital out of it for the movement. We shall become stronger through it, get more strength, and through the new strength again move forward.

My impression of the Sultan is that he is a weak, cowardly, but thoroughly well-meaning person. I think he is neither treacherous nor cruel, but a deeply unhappy prisoner, in whose name a thieving, infamous and dishonest *camarilla* commits the most shameful acts.

If I did not have to worry about the Zionist movement, I should go away from there and write an article which would give the poor prisoner his liberty. Abdul Hamid Khan II is a collective name for the most rascally band of thieves which ever made a land insecure and unhappy. I never ever dreamed of the possibility of such a gang of felons. The dishonesty and bribery which begin at the door of the palace and wind up only at the foot of the throne are probably not the worst. Everything is business, and every official is a thief. At least, I hear this on every side, and from what I know of the way things are done, I do not believe this to be a calumny.——

His Majesty the Sultan asks through Ibrahim[35] and Izzet[36] what would happen to the citizenship of those Jews who in one form or another would immigrate to Turkey.

"They can come to us," said Izzet Bey, in his barbarous French, "but they must become Turkish subjects. For instance, if you buy up the bonds of the Public Debt,

[35]Ibrahim, first secretary to the Sultan.
[36]Izzet Bey, second secretary to the Sultan.

the buyers must be subjects of His Imperial Majesty. The same is true of those who come as colonists. They must not only become Turkish subjects, but must renounce their previous citizenship, and get a statement from their previous governments testifying to their withdrawal from that citizenship."

"And they must accept military service," said Ibrahim, "if His Majesty calls them to the colors."

"Under those conditions we could receive the Jews of all countries," said Izzet, friendly as a hyena.

I thought to myself: *"Eine gute Kränk!"* It would suit Messrs. Izzet and his consorts down to the ground, if I were to bring rich Jews and poor Jews here to be robbed. But this was not the moment to raise objections to a pair of blackguards from whom we could later buy every paragraph in the charter.

I therefore said I was very happy to come under the glorious sceptre of Abdul Hamid, and declared myself ready to discuss the matter in detail.

Herzl now sets about the task. He has received from the Ministers of the Sultan an offer for the unification of the debt. His present task, however, is to interest financiers and to hold the possibility of the loan before the Sultan, in the hope of obtaining the charter.

Toward the end of May Herzl again sees the Grand Duke of Baden. He goes to Paris to push the matter of financing the Turkish debt. His understanding with the Turkish authorities is a vague one, and he counts on this fact to help tide over the long period that must elapse before he can organize the financial end of his combination.

June 2, in Paris.

I made no specific demands in Constantinople. I only spoke of my efforts. I can therefore say, three weeks later: My Jews are united in principle, but they want to have some assurance in advance—e.g., the Charter!

London, July 11, 1901.

In view of the hopelessness of interesting the rich Jews of Paris—or of anywhere else—Marmorek and Nordau have thought of trying to get money from the American Croesus philanthropist, Carnegie. Nordau believes he can clear the way to him by an introduction through the American Ambassador, Porter. But Porter was not in Paris.

Herzl keeps hunting for new possibilities again and again.

September 23, 1901.

In my chess game there figure at present Cecil Rhodes (whom I am to meet after his return from Scotland), Roosevelt[37] (through Gottheil), the King of England (through the Bishop of Ripon), the Czar (through General Von Hesse), etc.

Nothing happens. In December the Fifth Congress takes place in Basle. Herzl does not give any description of it until a week later.

THE FIFTH CONGRESS

January 5, 1902.

The change brought about by the passage of time shows itself most clearly in this: that it is only now, at this late date, that I set down my impressions of the Congress.

[37]Theodore Roosevelt, President of the United States.

From the evening of my arrival on the 25th of December until the moment of my departure on New Year's Eve, one discussion after the other. Sessions from 10 A.M. till 4 A.M. the next morning. In between, loose ends to tie up, insults to smooth over, etc.

On the morning of the first day I sent the telegram to the Sultan and on the evening of the second day I had the answer. I trembled up to the moment I got it. Up till that point he could still deny the beginnings of our relationship. But he fell for this completely. With this wire, handed to me by the telegraph office of Basle, my position is attested and regulated.

My delegates did not seem to appreciate the full value of the telegram. They understand nothing. They overrate the trivial, and underrate the important.

But it is enough that I know it.

Of less political value, but of infinitely higher moral value, was the official letter of greeting from the government of Basle.

The gentlemen of the Greater Actions Committee also made things difficult for me in the matter of the *baksheesh* which I have always had Wolffsohn, Kremenetzky, Kokesch, etc., hand out in exchange for a receipt.

Some of them acted as though I had been swindled out of the money. Also the Bank directors did not seem to like the idea of approving the amount we had spent toward getting the charter (Receipt Wolffsohn, N.). They would have done it if I had insisted, but then it would have been considered a "secret" and therefore would have got around quickly. Against this cowardice and stupidity I could do nothing other than throw the whole thing open in the Congress. To this end I used the oppositionist Farbstein, making his resolution my point of departure.

Naturally everything went through smoothly.

The directors and advisers could not understand the procedure, and they breathed more easily when it was over.

Zangwill and Cowen are active in London, trying to get together the right men for Herzl. Their latest move is to try and interest Lord Suffields and the financial group. Herzl writes them the details of his plan. In the midst of all these failures and worries the following strange entry occurs.

January 24, 1902.

Zionism was the Sabbath of my life.

I believe that my influence as a leader is based on the fact that while as man and writer I had so many faults, and committed so many blunders and mistakes, as a leader in Zionism I have remained pure of heart and quite selfless.

It is marvelous how far my thoughts reach out when I awake too early in the morning. Then I solve many of the problems of the present, and glimpse some of the problems of eternity.

This morning I thought about the human body, of which we know so little. Doctors have the professional blindness of dulled experts.

What a marvelous machine it is, the human body. A chemical laboratory, a power-house. Every movement, voluntary or involuntary, full of secrets and marvels. What gases and liquids are produced in it, harmful and useful. That is why I believe in the serum theory. Just as it produces poisons, so the body of the animal also produces antidotes, which as time progresses will certainly be discovered.

Early in February Herzl is called to Constantinople by Ibrahim Bey, in order to give details of his proposals. The call comes at a bad time for Herzl.

February 8, 1902.

With my head filled with worries, with my wife sick, I had to write, yesterday, a feuilleton on Japanese players. It reminds me of the time when I was writing the *Judenstaat* in Paris, and then from that had to go to the Chamber in order to report a session which was justly forgotten the next day.

And my feuilleton is quite good, at that.

BOOK TEN

February 17. *Constantinople.*

(*in the railway carriage beyond Verciorova.*)

FRAGRANT ORIENTAL LANDSCAPE ON THE DANUBE. GLEAMS of opal in the water, a weary delicately glowing mirror.

Slept badly; but now I'm going to the enigmatic East with an improved morning temper.

February 17. *Constantinople.*

The day began well and ended badly.

I finished my letter in reply to the Sultan, and then went to Yildiz somewhat delayed.

I handed my letter to Ibrahim, who then translated it into Turkish for the Sultan with the help of the second ceremonial minister Ghalib Bey. He had been commissioned to make a literal translation.——

Then we went in to lunch.

Izzet Bey read my answer through and with his habitual sharpness requested that I explain the Ottoman-Jewish Colonization Company. Was it to have the choice of the places to be colonized, where the Jews could buy land and settle in communities?

"Yes," I replied. "That is indispensable. After all, we're not concerned with individual protection which we have already in all civilized countries—but with national protection."

Their Excellencies asked what I understood by that.

I explained: a great demonstration in our favor, such as an invitation to immigrate without restrictions.

Then Izzet went to the Sultan with my letter.

While we were waiting Ibrahim and Ghalib were very enthusiastic about the coming happy events; how it would be if the Jews were to come. They dreamed aloud of the advancement of agriculture and industry, about banks that would not be in the service of foreigners, etc.

But then Izzet returned with the Sultan's answer, and that was unfavorable. The Sultan would open his empire to all Jews who became Turkish subjects but the districts for settlement were to be determined in each case by the government, and Palestine was to be excluded. The Otto-man-Jewish Company could colonize in Mesopotamia, Syria, Anatolia and anywhere else, but not in Palestine!

A charter without Palestine! I refused at once.

February 21, 1902.

A wire from Greenberg[38] this evening: certain London papers have published articles with the statement that I have obtained the Charter.

[38] J. L. Greenberg, English Zionist who was active as a repre-sentative of Herzl in negotiating with British officials over El Arish.

BOOK ELEVEN

The negotiations with Turkey continue. Herzl never dismissed that country from his mind, but always continued negotiations.

May 3, 1902. From a Letter to Izzet.

DEAR EXCELLENCY:

I FEAR THAT PEOPLE HAVE BEEN WORKING AGAINST ME a little, and that I have been slightly neglected.——

But I think I have found a way of replying to those who may be presenting me in an unfavorable light. The way is simply to offer a great service to His Imperial Majesty. This will counteract the unhealthy spirit.

In a word: create a Jewish university, embracing all the sciences in their highest and most modern form, and create this model university in your country! The costs will present no difficulties.

What do you think of it? If H.I.M. wishes to summon me it will be possible to talk of these and other things at the same time.

Please accept, dear Excellency, the assurance of my sincere regard.

Dr. Th. H.

Herzl received an invitation to appear before a British Royal Commission on Alien Immigration.

June 9, 1902.

What I need now is the condensation of my organization—the liquefaction of the gaseous quantity which is called the Zionist movement.

To that end I shall pursue the following paths:

1. By my evidence before the Royal Commission I shall make clear to the Government that it is on the horns of a dilemma: one horn is the abandonment of the glorious principle of asylum, the other the lack of protection of home labor. My way out—if they ask for it—would be the founding of the Chartered Company for Cyprus.

At the same time I shall make a semi-official attempt to get in touch with Lord R. He is in a furious rage against me—perhaps this is the psychological moment for the conclusion of peace. When he was asked in the Commission why he was opposed to calling me, he said that I was a demagogue, a windbag.

2. I shall try to build up a mining concern for the exploitation of the Turkish Mines.

London, the night of the ninth to the tenth of June 1902.

When I returned to the hotel from the theatre I found this wire from my wife:

"Papa very ill. Come Vienna at once."

It is death. I saw that immediately.

Two hours were taken up with getting train information, packing. The rest of the night will be harder to pass.

This book must record it. I believe that toward my good father, who did so much for me, I have always been a faithful, grateful and respectful son.

How much he went through with me! How he sustained me, comforted me, after he had educated and kept me for so long.

The journeys, on which I learned so much, I owe to him.

And now I am not at home when he closes his eyes. What an enduring help he was to me, what a counselor. Like a tree, he stood by me. Now the tree is gone.

On July 5th Herzl is again in London; he meets Rothschild. The latter is anxious to censor in advance the evidence which Herzl will give before the Royal Commission.

July 5.

In England, said Rothschild, there will never be any anti-Semitism, etc. In France it was a different matter, etc.

He does not believe in Zionism.

We should never get Palestine, etc. He is an Englishman and wants to remain one. He "desires" me to say this and that to the Alien Commission, and not to say this and the other.

At this point the business became too stupid for me. I had interrupted him a couple of times. But now I began to flout him in such a way that he was dazed and kept his mouth shut.

"I shall tell the Commission what I think proper and the truth as I see it. That is my habit, and I shall cling to it now, too."

It was false, I said, that the Powers were against our going to Palestine. I have influenced Germany and Russia in our favor. England, I thought, would have nothing against it. I was *persona grata* with the Sultan.

"Yes," he threw in, "the Sultan is naturally friendly to you, because you are Dr. Herzl of the *Neue Freie Presse*."

"It is false," I cried. "The *Neue Freie Presse* has nothing to do with it. The publishers are deadly enemies of my plan. The word Zionism has not been printed in that paper until this day. I never had anything to do with the Sultan in connection with the *Neue Freie Presse.*"

He said further that Arnold White[39] and Gordon[40] had called me as a Crown witness in order that I should support them and they could say: "Dr. Herzl is certainly the best of Jews, and he states that a Jew can never become an Englishman."

"It would be stupid and arrogant of me," I said, "to read the Commission a lecture on the characteristics of the real Englishman. I shall simply say what terrible misery there is in the East, and that these people must either get away or perish. The need in Rumania has been known to us since 1897; the Congress petition received no attention. In Galicia it is perhaps even worse. There are seven hundred thousand people there in misery. They will also begin to move."

My Lord said: "I hope you are not going to say that to the Commission. Or else we shall have restrictions."

At this point I became adamant. "Certainly I shall say it. You can count on that."

Whereupon his jaw dropped, he rang, and called his brother Leopold.

To him he repeated what had been said, and added that in my opinion Jewish charity had merely become a machine for the suppression of the cry of misery.——

[39]Arnold White, author of the "Modern Jew".

[40]Major W. E. Evans-Gordon, M.P., member of the British Alien Immigration Committee.

BOOK TWELVE

July 17, in a railway carriage between Calais and Paris.

PRIVATE AND CONFIDENTIAL.

Dated July 21, Alt-Aussee.

Dear Lord Rothschild,

I was unable to answer your letter of the 15th in London during the rush of my departure, because, as you say yourself, my suggestions concerning colonization require lengthier study.

I am quite in agreement with that. It was also my idea that colonization could begin only in the early spring —February or March—during the time of the summer planting, because that is the shortest time to the first harvest. It would be necessary, of course, to make sure of the terrain in the autumn and use the winter for preparations, the details of which I have long since worked out.

I would be so happy if I did not have to interpret your answer as a refusal. Who can help our poor people if not you?

You are a good man—today, after coming to know you, I am convinced of it. Be a great man as well.

The undertaking can be assured of success only if it is carried out with sufficient means and with possibilities of expansion.

It is not difficult to count on 16 million pounds for a subway from Piccadilly to Cornhill. Funds amounting to 10 million pounds for some industrial enterprise or other are not fabulous sums in these American times. Can it be that under Lord Rothschild's leadership a land-company which is to rid the world once and for all of the tormenting Jewish question will not be able to collect this amount?

I know very well what causes the confusion here: the matter seems to be of too philanthropic a nature for one to deal with and present it in a businesslike way.

But it is precisely through this undertaking that you may gain immortal fame for yourself.

As I understand you, Milord, you would not object at all if one were to presume on your presenting 10 or 20 thousand pounds for a relief campaign. I have heard it said that you give away over 100,000 pounds annually.

But in this case you need give no money at all, not a penny—you need only lend your authority, your influence, your power to an enterprise which will probably be profitable.

Have you so low an opinion of the prestige of your House that you can for a moment doubt the collection of 10 million pounds among the Jews of the entire world, if you place yourself at the head of the cause?

Your cousins in Paris could no longer lead such an undertaking. They are indirectly ruled by E. A. Drumont,[41] and woe unto them if they do not behave like French patriots in the financial affairs of the Russian government, that is turning our people into pariahs.

[41]Leader of the anti-Semites in France. 1877–1917.

But your situation, Milord, is quite different—at any rate today, before anti-Semitism has penetrated into England.

At this time you can still move freely. You might even bring it to the immediate attention of your government that you are able to strengthen English influence by settling large numbers of our people at the intersection of Egyptian and Indo-Persian interests in the Mediterranean.

How long do you believe the importance of that region will remain unnoticed? And then we clever Jews, who are always outwitted, will once again be too late. The thing can be done: swiftly and on a large scale, by means of the Land and Commerce Company, the characteristics of which I sketched out to you. Hirsch's enterprise was an ostentatious plaything with no possibilities. Communal life does not consist merely of agriculture. The part of these millions that has not yet been dissipated will inevitably have to flow into a comprehensive settlement project. But I have as little desire to depend on that as on other "philanthropies."

The Land Company can be successful only if it is based not on "*rachmones*" but on economic interest. I may succeed in acquiring some financially valuable concessions, in which case you will hear from me again.

I shall leave for Constantinople tomorrow morning. I do not know how long I shall remain there. If there is anything you think I should know please communicate with me through Mr. Greenberg, 80 Chancery Lane, who always has my address.

Your very obedient
Herzl.

August 5, 1902.

If I can do nothing with Chamberlain,[42] I shall try Italy.

Ehrenpreis, the Rabbi of Sofia, told me, while he traveled part of the way with me, that when the King of Italy was in Sofia he asked the then Italian attaché, Polacco, about our movement. Naturally the Jew Polacco knew less than the king.

[42]Joseph Chamberlain, British Colonial Minister.

BOOK THIRTEEN

October 23, 1902.

SPOKE YESTERDAY WITH THE FAMOUS RULER OF ENGLAND, Joe Chamberlain. An hour. I explained everything that I wanted to do. And he listened well. Unfortunately my voice shook at the beginning, which made me angry while I was speaking.

In a few minutes it was going better, and I spoke calmly and convincingly, as well as my muddled English permitted me to.

I laid the entire Jewish question before the immobile mask which is Joe Chamberlain. My relations to Turkey, etc.

"I am in negotiation with the Sultan," I said in English. "But you know what Turkish negotiations are. If you want to buy a carpet, first you must drink half a dozen cups of coffee and smoke a hundred cigarettes. Then you discuss family stories, and from time to time you speak a few words again about the carpet. Now I have time to negotiate, but my people have not. They are starving in the Pale. I must bring them immediate help." And so on.

The mask smiled at the carpet story.

I then passed on to the subject of the territory which I wanted from England: Cyprus, El Arish and the Sinai Peninsula.

First he said he could speak only about Cyprus. The rest concerned not him but the Foreign Office. But as for Cyprus, the situation was that there were Greeks and Mohammedans living there, and he could not push them out for the sake of new immigrants. On the contrary he must as a matter of duty stand on their side. And if the Greeks—perhaps with the support lent them by Greece and Russia—were to oppose Jewish immigration, the difficulties would be complete. He personally had nothing against the Jews, on the contrary. And if by some chance he were to have a drop of Jewish blood in his veins he would be proud of it. But, there you are, he didn't have a drop.

In the meantime he was prepared to help if he could; he was sympathetic to the idea of Zionism, etc.——

To which I replied that not everything after all was made public in politics but only the results or whatever was necessary for discussion. And I explained my plan to him of having a movement created for us in Cyprus before anything else. We must be invited to come there. I would have that prepared by a half dozen emissaries. If we were to establish the Jewish Eastern Company with 5 million pounds for Sinai and El Arish the Cypriotes would begin to desire the rain of gold on their own island. The Mohammedans would move off and the Greeks would sell their lands with pleasure and remove to Athens or Crete.

He seemed to be pleased with the idea. But he could say nothing about El Arish and Sinai. The government would want to hear the opinion of Lord Cromer,[43] in whom they had great faith.

It was a pity that Lord Cromer was no longer there. He was back in Egypt already.

[43]Lord Cromer, British High Commissioner to Egypt.

"I can send someone there," I said.

"But you must speak to the Foreign Office."

"Help me do that, Mr. Chamberlain. I am leaving the day after tomorrow."

He thought about it and gave me an appointment for today at 12:15, when I would see Lord Lansdowne.[44]

Was it before or after this that I drew El Arish for him on a sheet of paper lying on his desk? And with it my idea about the Haifa hinterland, that is, that I would impel the Turks to come to an agreement more quickly with me by turning up in the waters of the Nile. Then I might get the Haifa Region more cheaply.

At this the smoothly shaven mask laughed again and let the monocle fall.

But he had no idea where El Arish was, and so we went to a large table where he picked out an atlas from among some other big books and found Egypt. While doing this he said: "We would have the same difficulty with the inhabitants in Egypt too."

"No," I said, "we will not go to Egypt. We have been there."

Then he laughed again, this time bent all the way over the book. For the first time now he fully understood me and my desire to get a gathering-place for the Jewish people in the neighborhood of Palestine.

The land is empty in El Arish and Sinai. England can give it to us. For this it would reap the gratitude of 10 million Jews and an increase in power. I told him all this and it made an impression on him. And I concluded:

"Would you agree to our founding a Jewish colony on the Sinai Peninsula?"

[44]Lord Lansdowne, British Foreign Minister.

"Yes," he said, "if Lord Cromer approves of it."

So this is the first thing I have to attend to.

He excused himself and we made an appointment for today.

November 7, Vienna.

I am completely worn out and have had to relax.

During the annual conference and everything connected with it I exhausted myself to such an extent that I have had every possible heart condition since Sunday.

I've been dragging myself around the whole week, incapable of writing two lines.

Today I finally told the *Neue Freie Presse* that I was ill.

I sent Greenberg to Egypt. I have just received a telegram from this admirable fellow from Cairo, where he arrived the day before yesterday, that he is returning tomorrow morning, "everything all right", and will be here Wednesday.

Is it possible that we are on the verge of the completion of a charter—an English one—and of the foundation of the Jewish State?

My exhausted powers make it appear credible.

December 22, Vienna

I received Lord Lansdowne's reply yesterday, written by Sir T. H. Sanderson,[45] an historic document.

Lord Cromer states that the project for the Sinai Peninsula would be possible—if the Commission finds the actual situation possible. The Egyptian government would only demand Ottoman sovereignty and an annual

[45]Sir T. H. Sanderson, Secretary to the British Foreign Minister.

levy for the maintenance of order externally and internally.

I shall dispatch the commission: Marmorek, the architect, Kessler,[46] the engineer, Professor Warburg,[47] one of the Palestinian agriculturists, and the geographer from the Sudan recommended by Cromer.

I shall make a great point of Ottoman sovereignty (guaranteed by England) to the Sultan, and demand a slice of Palestine in return.

I shall promise the Egyptian government to collect the annual levy, and keep the promise, if the Governor of the Egyptian province of Judea is elected by the colonists for ten or seven years and merely confirmed by the Khedive. Or put up by the English government and nominated by the Khedive.

Anglo-Egyptian officers may be in command of the police power, and the ranks will be filled by our men.

On the basis of these achievements Lord Rothschild must get me the money of the ICA—at least two or three million pounds for the Jewish Eastern Company—the rest by public subscription.

December 30, Vienna.

It occurred to me today between nightfall and morning:

We might be able to make the wilderness fruitful with the Nile!

To be sure a simple transmission would probably be impossible because of the Suez Canal; it would have

---

[46]Leopold Kessler, member of the Actions Committee.

[47]Prof. Otto Warburg, Botanica-Berlin University, President of the World Zionist Organization 1911–1920.

to be pumped over by means of elevated pipelines or deep down under the earth. The latter seems to me much the easier.

Such an aqueduct might cost millions and still not be too dear.

Or mud (dredged out mud) could be shipped in boats, but instead of being dumped into the sea be sent to El Arish.

The expedition is leaving Trieste the 29th of this month.

I am settling all the details with Cook, provisioning, etc. I am now studying the maps of the country.

From Book Fourteen we learn that, in January 15, 1903, Herzl is again in London, organizing the expedition which will go to El Arish to report on the possibilities of colonization. On March 22nd Herzl is already on his way to Cairo, to enter upon the final negotiations.

BOOK FIFTEEN

March 29, Cairo

The poverty of the fellahs by the wayside indescribable.

I intend to think of the fellahs as well, once I have the power.

April 27, 1903. London

Saw Chamberlain yesterday afternoon.

He received me cordially as an old acquaintance.——

I gave a report and referred him to the report of the Commission, which I had sent him the day before and which lay in front of him.

"It's not a favorable report," he said.

"Yes," I said, "it's a very poor country; but we want to make something of it."

"I saw a country for you on my trip," said the great Chamberlain, "and that's Uganda. It's hot on the coast, but towards the interior the climate becomes excellent for Europeans. You can plant sugar and cotton there. So I thought to myself, There's a country for Dr. Herzl. But he only wants to go to Palestine or near it."

"Yes, I must," I replied. "We must have the foundations in or near Palestine. Later on we might settle Uganda also, because we have masses of people who are ready to emigrate, But we must build on a national foundation, and for this reason we need a political attraction in El Arish. But in Egypt they don't understand that. At any rate I couldn't explain myself as distinctly there as here."——

We spoke back and forth.

"In Asia Minor," said Chamberlain, "our interests are getting less and less. There's going to be a settlement there some day between France, Germany, and Russia whereas we are being drawn away more and more to more distant points. I wonder what would be the fate of your Jewish colony in Palestine in that case, even if you succeeded in establishing it?"

I said: "I think that then we'll really have prospects for the first time, because then we shall serve as a small buffer state. We shall become one not from the good-will but from the jealousy of the powers. And if we're under the Union Jack in El Arish, then our Palestine will also fall within the British sphere of influence."——

Towards the end of April, Herzl is in London, where he again speaks with Chamberlain, and with Lord Landsdowne. He is in Vienna on May 8th when he gets the telegram from Goldsmid which tells him that the whole plan has fallen through.

Vienna, May 13, 1903.

Letter from Goldsmid, under date May 6th. The explanation: "Sir William Garstein declares that we would need five times as much water as Stephens estimated; also the laying down of the syphons would interfere for several weeks with the traffic on the Suez Canal."——

BOOK SIXTEEN

May 16, 1903.

I CONSIDERED THE SINAI MATTER SO COMPLETELY READY, that I would no longer buy a family vault in the *Döblinger* cemetery, where my father rests provisionally. Now I consider the matter so completely smashed, that I have already chosen the family vault.

May 19, 1903. From a letter to Plehve:

Now I have been informed by very serious people that there is a means of calming the hopeless mood of our people immediately, and that would be for His Majesty the Czar to accord me an audience. This fact alone would result in instantaneous appeasement even though not a word concerning the content of the interview were to reach the public.

I am accustomed to justifying such confidence, as is indicated by the fact that the contents of my repeated conversations with His Majesty the German Kaiser and the Sultan have never come to the public.

I could use the occasion of my audience, if it is granted, to provide the government of His Majesty the Czar with all the information desired about our movement and petition it for further assistance.

Some years ago I described the aims of our Zionist movement to the Czar in a memorandum composed in French, which His Royal Highness the Grand Duke of

Baden had the kindness to transmit, and for which I obtained His Majesty's thanks.——

June 4, 1903. *From a letter to Reinach (of ICA)*

——One more thing, this one of less importance. The purchase of some land in the Valley of Jezreel has been proposed to us. The vendor is a M. Soursouk, I think of Beirut. He has been quoted to me as saying: "Either the ICA or the Zionists will buy this land from me." So it would appear that certain speculators wish to profit by what they believe to be our rivalry. It would be easy to cripple manoeuvres of this sort by giving each other mutual warnings. For my part I shall keep you informed of the above even without reciprocity. I shall let you know at what price land is being offered to us in Palestine. If you don't breathe a word of it to anyone we may be able to expose one or another of the shameful speculations you've spoken to me about.

M. Soursouk is asking 25 francs a dunam for land the value of which, according to our reports, wouldn't be more than from 15 to 18 francs.

If you wish to buy we shall withdraw. If you do not wish to, state this clearly to M. Soursouk[48] so that we may be able to buy at a cheaper price.

The Russian episode now intervenes, his original hope of seeing the Czar is disappointed. The Russian trip is taken against the advice of several members of the Actions Committee. The rift between Herzl and these members—chiefly the Russians—widens as the *Uganda* question comes to the fore. He reports the following in the *Diaries*, shortly before he leaves for Russia. And it is in Russia that Herzl receives the news of the English offer of *Uganda.*

[48]Soursouk, a Syrian who owned large areas of land in Palestine.

Vienna, June 11, 1903.

I called a meeting of the Actions Committee in my house, and laid before them my new Portuguese African Plan. Kokesch raised his eyebrows and declared sharply against it. Kahn was for it. Kremenetzky saw the correctness of my explanation—namely, that we could ask for Palestine with more strength, and more pressure, if we had a publicly secured, legally assured place to gather in. Marmorek accepted my view only to the extent that it meant the creation of something which could be exchanged for Palestine.

BOOK SEVENTEEN

August 10, Petersburg.

IT IS ONLY TODAY, AFTER THE COMPLETION OF THE MOST pressing matters, that I can manage to describe my encounters with the chief figures of present-day Russia.

Saw Plehve the morning of the day before yesterday.——

"Although the Jewish question is not vital for us it is nevertheless rather important. And we are endeavoring to clear it up in the best way possible. I have accorded you this interview in order to discuss the matter with you before your congress in Basle, as was your wish. I understand of course that your position in this question differs from that of the Russian government, and first of all I should like to explain our point of view. The Russian state desires the utmost homogeneity in its population, although we realize that we cannot do away with all variations of faith and language.

"For example, we must admit that the older Scandinavian culture is maintaining itself in Finland as something fixed. But we demand from all peoples within our realm, including the Jews, that they conceive of the Russian state as the unchangeable foundation of our existence. We wish to assimilate the Jews to us, and have two ways leading to this goal: that of higher education and that of economic advancement. Those who have achieved a certain degree of success in both these fields and who, because of their education and prosperity, may safely be assumed to be faithful to the existing regime, are accorded civil rights by us. But this assimilation which we desire is taking place very slowly.

"In any case we can permit only a limited number of Jews to share in the benefits of higher education, because otherwise we would soon have no offices left for Christians. I am quite aware of the fact that the economic condition of the Jews in the pale of settlement is bad. I admit also that they live there as though in a ghetto, but it is nevertheless a large area, with thirteen provinces. The situation has become still worse recently because of the Jews going over to the insurrectionary parties. We were sympathetic to your Zionist movement as long as it helped to further emigration. You don't have to begin justifying the movement to me. You are preaching to a convert. But since the congress in Minsk we have noticed a change in the higher-ups. There is less talk of Palestinian Zionism than of culture, organization and Jewish nationalism. That doesn't suit us. We have noticed in particular that your chief people in Russia—who are very respected individuals in their circles—are not really adherents of your Viennese Committee. In reality only Ussishkin supports you in Russia."——

Afternoon of Saturday the 8th.

Maximov[49] and Katzenelson went with me to Pavlovsk, a sort of Russian Potsdam, where General Kireyev lives in the castle of a grand duchess as court marshal. Kireyev, Aksakov's successor, is the head of the Slavophiles. But though I had imagined him to myself as a wild bear up to

[49]Maximov, a Russian Liberal.

then, there I found myself in the presence of a charming old cavalier, elegant, kindly, modern and informed, who speaks German, French and English excellently, and knows a great deal besides.

While I spoke I liked looking into his fine blue eyes. With his white equestrian's moustache he was very charming. I won him to our idea.

Sunday the 9th I went to the islands to see Witte.——

He began by asking me who I was (in spite of my having been introduced!) and when I had given a brief sketch of myself and the cause—presented from the government's point of view—he began speaking at some length:

"Do not call this point of view that of the government. It is only that of some individuals within the government. You want to take the Jews away? Are you a Hebrew? Whom am I speaking with, anyhow?"

"I am a Hebrew and the head of the Zionist movement."

"And whatever we say is between ourselves?"

"Absolutely!" I said so energetically that from then he let himself go unrestrainedly. He began with a description of the Jewish question in Russia.——

The Emperor had "honest prejudices" against the Jews. The Czar's honesty could not be called into question because he stood above everything else. The anti-Semitic prejudices of the Emperor were chiefly of a religious nature.——

"It is difficult," he continued, "to come to the defense of the Jews, because then it is immediately said that one has been bought. But that has no effect on me. I have sufficient courage. Also my reputation as an honorable man is too firmly established for any one to touch me. But faint-hearted and pushing people let themselves be influenced by this and prefer to turn against the Jews. And recently something weighty has been added: the participation of the Jews in insurrectionary movements. Whereas only 7 million of the 136 million of our population are Jews, their share in the revolutionary parties is about 50%."

"What circumstances do you ascribe this to, your Excellency?"

"I think it is the fault of our government. The Jews are too oppressed. I used to tell the deceased Emperor Alexander III: 'Your Majesty, if it were possible to drown the 6 or 7 million Jews in the Black Sea I should be in complete accord with it. But since it is not possible then you must let them live.' And that has remained my opinion. I am against further measures of oppression."

"But the present state of affairs? Do you believe that the present state of affairs can be maintained?"

"Certainly. Russia has powers of resistance which are not conceived of abroad. We can endure the greatest calamities for a very long time."

"I am not speaking of Russia but of the Jews. Do you believe that the Jews can continue to endure this desperate condition for a long time?"

"Where is the way out?"

I proceeded to explain this, answering all his well-known objections with my long-prepared arguments.

But I had met his objections before among rich, anti-Zionist, Jewish financiers, who had clearly been instructing him about Zionism. Even the old anecdote about the ambassador's appointment was there. He said: "Twenty years ago I was in Marienbad together with a Jewish deputy from Hungary. What was his name, anyhow?"

"Wahrmann?"

"Yes. Even at that time people were already speaking about setting up a Jewish state in Palestine, and Herr Wahrmann said that if it ever came to that he would want to be the Austrian ambassador in Jerusalem."

Clearly Wahrmann had said "Jewish ambassador in Budapest." M. Witte related the anecdote badly.

Then I seized his counter-arguments by the throat exactly as they were presented and annihilated them. He kept on admitting more and more that I was right. He only balked at the Holy Places (like all the Jewish bankers).

Not a single anti-Semite had stumbled on it before; only he, the *"Judeaophile."*

Finally he asked what I wanted from the government.

"Encouragement."

"Mais on donne aux juifs des encouragements à l'emigration. Par example les coups de pied." (But we do encourage the Jews to emigrate. By kicking them, for example.)

I answered this stupid piece of brutality by drawing myself up coldly and quietly, and icily replied:

"I do not wish to speak of this type of encouragement. It is well known."

And I explained the three points of my memorandum to Plehve.

Witte finally admitted that my solution was good if it could be applied. I requested by way of support for the movement that he lift the ban on the shares of the Jewish Colonial Bank. He promised to on condition that we set up a branch in Russia (which is just what we want ourselves), so that its conduct could be supervised. I accepted the condition at once.

August 17, *in a railway carriage between Thorn and Posen.*

I shall never forget yesterday, the day in Vilna. This is no banquet phrase.

My arrival in the Russian-Polish city in the morning was the signal for ovations. I dislike that sort of thing.——

Suddenly at night on the veranda of the home where I dined, appeared poor boys and girls who had walked two hours to see me at dinner.

Herzl's report of the Sixth Congress [the Uganda Congress] is brief. It follows almost in full.

August 31, 1903.

The great, difficult Sixth Congress is over.

When, exhausted, I returned after the closing session, with my friends Zangwill, Nordau and Cowen,[50] to Cowen's room, to sit down round a bottle of mineral water, I said to them:

"I will tell you now what my speech is going to be to the Seventh Congress, if I live till then.

"By then I shall either have Palestine, or shall have convinced myself of the absolute hopelessness of all further effort.

[50]Joseph Cowen, one of the first English Zionists, later Secretary of the English Zionist Federation.

"In the latter case my speech will be as follows:

" 'It was not possible. Our final objective has not been reached. But an intermediary objective is possible: this land on which we can settle our suffering masses, with a national basis and self-government. I do not believe that we ought to withhold this relief from these unfortunate ones.

" 'But I understand that with this situation a decisive split has entered our movement, and this split passes through my person. Although in the beginning I thought only of a Jewish State—no matter where—I later raised the flag of Zion, and I myself became a "lover of Zion." Palestine is the only land where our people can achieve tranquillity. But immediate help must be given to hundreds of thousands.

" 'In order to heal this split there is only one thing to be done: I must withdraw from the leadership. If you desire it, I shall still guide the discussions of this Congress, and at the end you can choose two Actions Committees, one for East Africa and one for Palestine. I shall not permit myself to be elected to either. But I shall never refuse my advice to those who take up the work—if they ask me for it.

" 'By that which I have done, I have not made Zionism poorer, but Jewry richer.

" 'Adieu.' "

The last months of Herzl's life are taken up with three-fold negotiations: England, Russia, and ICA. The Revolt of the Russian Zionists embitters him. His last important journey is to Rome, in January, 1904.

BOOK EIGHTEEN

January 20, in a railway carriage outside of Florence.

Very busy in Vienna till the last moment, then a 24-hour respite in Venice.

A very blue Monday.

In the evening I felt too dull to put on my dinner-jacket for the 1½ Englishmen in the Grand Hotel, so I went into Bauer's Austrian beer house.

When I entered somebody bowed to me from a corner where a group was sitting. I didn't recognize him immediately. Then a waiter came and asked me whether I was Herzl from Vienna.

In order to have some peace I wanted to say no at first, but then I admitted it anyhow.

And then—the painter and papal Count Lippay came to my table.

In this way something was begun that may have great consequences.

After five minutes Lippay said to me: "Come to Rome, and I'll introduce you to the Pope."

He was obviously doing this out of *braggadocio*.

I didn't answer : "I was just going to ask it of you," but "we might get together on that."——

January 23, Rome.

I had my audience with the King today.——

I can't think how, we got to talking about Palestine.

"I know it quite well," he said. "I've been there several

times. Also just at the time my father was assassinated. The country is very Jewish already. It must and will come to you, it's only a question of time. After you have half a million Jews there."

"They are not permitted to enter, Sire!"

"Oh my, everything goes with some baksheesh."

"But I shouldn't want that at all. Our project means investments, improvements; I don't want to have those made as long as it doesn't belong to us."

He laughed and said an Italian word, meaning something like: "Of course, those would be improvements *in casa di altri* (in some one else's house)."

"First I'd like to have the Sultan behind it."

"The only thing that has any effect on him," said the King, "is money. If you promise him half the produce of the Jordan Valley he'll let you have it."

"Yes, but we need autonomy."

"He won't want to hear anything about that. He doesn't like the word."

"What it stands for is enough for me, Sire! It can be called anything at all. I shall take the liberty of saying now what I am asking of your Grace."

He laughed: "Good, I'm listening!"

Then I showed him Plehve and the Grand Duke's letter, to show him how things had already been begun.——

I explained everything to him and finally asked:

"Sire, your personal intervention with the Sultan could help us a great deal. Write him a letter!"

He said: "I would be quite willing to, but I cannot do what I want. If I promise you something now and don't hold to it—that would be hardly the procedure of a gentleman. I must ask advice on it. Speak to Tittoni also (the Minister of the Exterior). I'm seeing him to-night, and I'll prepare him for your visit. I am only prom-ising you my good will, but not my action."——

I saw the Pope yesterday.——

I presented my request briefly, but he answered: "We cannot look with favor upon this movement. We cannot prevent the Jews from going to Jerusalem—but we can never favor it."——

"But, Holy Father, the Jews are having a terrible time. I do not know whether your Holiness is acquainted with the whole scope of this melancholy situation. We need a country for these persecuted people."

"Must it be Gerusalemme?"

"We are not asking for Jerusalem, but for Palestine, only the profane part of the country."

Saw the Minister of the Foreign Affairs Tittoni yester-day.

A slim, black, buttoned up frock coat. Over it a short gray full beard, an over-sized Roman nose and piercing policeman's eyes, which look out from behind peculiarly protruding swollen eye-lids.

The conversation lasted only ten minutes, but was excellent. The good King had arranged everything be-forehand. The King is just as clever and chivalrous as he is small. He had promised me nothing definite. But Tit-toni declared—obviously commissioned by the King—that he was ready to do everything possible. He wants to write the ambassador in Constantinople that he is to proceed together with the Russians. But of course the personal intervention of the King could be risked after it had been made certain that it would be accepted.

In the last few months Herzl was in touch with statesmen of England, Russia, Turkey and Italy. But the tempo of his work begins to die down. His last approach to the subject was a letter to Jacob Schiff, written March 30th. The entries into the *Diaries* are now very scattered. The last letter entered is the second one to Schiff, May 16, 1904.

May 16, 1904.

Dear Mr. Schiff:

"My friend, Dr. Katzenelson, came here from London, and reported that you have received him in the friendliest fashion. Please permit me to offer you my warmest thanks. Dr. K. also told me that he had given you a copy of my confidential instructions since I rely absolutely on your discretion.

"The matter is secret and must so remain, above all from the gentlemen of the ICA. From them I can expect anything rather than readiness to co-operate. Certainly there are among the directors of the ICA excellent people; but as a group they have always shown themselves hostile whenever a really great action for a really great need was touched on.

"I do not know why these gentlemen are ready to use up the money of Baron de Hirsch in small-change enterprises which represent everything rather than Jewish colonization. Were it not for the fact that our masses are perishing in filth and misery while this means of help goes unused, it would be possible to write humorous observations on the subject. For instance, the greatest enemy of a testament is its executor. Or, the relatives of Baron de Hirsch at least have this satisfaction, that the poor Jews, too, get nothing out of the money.

"However, I shall not permit the ICA and its mistakes to occupy me long. These gentlemen will come running after us when we no longer need them.

"You will know the general trend of my ideas through Dr. K. and my letter."

(Here the Diaries break off.)

(Herzl died July 3, 1904.)